The **Essential** Bu...

DATSU

240Z

1969-1973

Your marque expert:
Jon Newlyn

VELOCE PUBLISHING
THE PUBLISHER OF FINE AUTOMOTIVE BOOKS

www.veloce.co.uk

  Belvedere

First published in March 2018, by Veloce Publishing Limited, Veloce House, Parkway Farm Business Park, Middle Farm Way,
Poundbury, Dorchester, Dorset, DT1 3AR, England.
Telephone 01305 260068/Fax 01305 250479/email info@veloce.co.uk/web www.veloce.co.uk or www.velocebooks.com.
ISBN: 978-1-787112-02-5 UPC: 6-36847-01202-1 © Jon Newlyn and Veloce Publishing 2018. All rights reserved. With the

British Library Cataloguing in Publication Data – A catalogue record for this book is available from the British Library.
Typesetting, design and page make-up all by Veloce Publishing Ltd on Apple Mac. Printed and bound by Replika Press.

Introduction
– the purpose of this book

Background

The Datsun/Nissan 240Z (HS30) was launched to an unsuspecting world on 18th October 1969 at the Tokyo Motor Show; shipments began to the US in December 1969.

Datsun was an export name only; Nissan was used for Japan. In the Japanese Domestic Market (JDM), the Z was first known as the Fairlady Z – an S30 model with a 2-litre engine, which replaced the 2-litre Fairlady roadster. It wasn't until 1971 that the HS30 was available in Japan, known as a Fairlady 240Z. The Fairlady/Datsun roadster was built, in different guises, from 1959. The very first roadster, the S211, started with a 998cc engine, and all models were constructed with a separate body and chassis.

The 240Z was fundamentally different, being constructed as a monocoque (single shell), giving it strength and lightness. For the domestic market, there were three models with three engines: S30 – a new L20, designated L20A – a 1952cc, 12-valve straight six engine, SOHC, producing 115PS (85kW). There was also the fuel injected L20E, with 130PS (96kW). This was deemed necessary because of the stringent tax laws in Japan regarding engine size. PS30 – the S20 engine was a 1989cc, DOHC (designed by the former Prince engineers in the 1970s). It was a revised production variant of the 1966 Prince GR8 engine from Prince/Nissan's R380. It produced 160hp (120kW). HS30 from 1971 – the L24 was a 2393cc, 12-valve, straight-six SOHC engine, with twin SU carburettors, producing 151PS (110kW). Export markets got the HS30 L24 engine.

The all-new design, with echoes of the Jaguar E-type and Porsche 912, offered performance similar to either at a price equal to the MGBs and Triumph sports car models of the day. The model was sold in the USA for $3500, or about £1000.

The USA was the primary export target market for the 240Z, with nearly 150,000 sold over four years, compared to just over 11,000 for Canada, under 2500 for Australia, less than 2000 for the UK, and only 1000 for Germany, Holland and France.

Although the export market only had the L24 engine, it was offered with three gearbox types: a four- or five-speed manual, and a three-speed automatic. The four-speed, which seemed at odds with the type of driving done in America, was fitted to keep the price below the $3500 target. For the rest of the world, the five-speed was a standard fitment.

The steering was unassisted rack and pinion, and is heavy at parking speeds. The front suspension was of a strut design, taken and modified from the Bluebird (model 510) saloon. The rear independent suspension was unique to the Z, and provided great wheel location at the expense of space and noise. A British company, Race Head Services, based at Silverstone Circuit, produced modified Zs with gas-flowed heads and staged cams; these were called Samuris (it was either without the 'a' for copyright reasons, or it was misspelt!). It turned an already quick car (0-60 in 8 secs and 125mph) into a car that would humble most sports cars available at the time, with 0-60mph in 6 secs and a 140mph top speed.

The interior was spacious for two people, with ample luggage space. The 240Z was designed to cater for the generally larger European and American human frame. The dashboard was of a contoured design, with hooded and deeply

A pound and a half of legend.

Race Head Services – Silverstone, circa 1988.

recessed dials: two in front of the driver, and three dials atop the centre section.

This design has since become one of the staple features of the car, being carried forward to the current 370Z. There was a dealer option for air-conditioning – for the USA and JDM. For the European market, the heating system consisted simply of slider controls and a three-speed fan. The seats are thin with a built-in headrest, finished in PVC, designed to look like leather, and although slim in design, are surprisingly comfortable over long distances. The 240Z filled a gap for a cheap, dependable sports car – the value being more obvious in the American market than in the UK. The 240Z was priced within $200 of the MGB in America, compared to the first UK 240Zs retailing at £2238, against a Ford Capri 3.0 at £1700, and the Jaguar E-type at £2800. It was almost double the price of an MGB.

Success in various world rallies set the reputation for the 240Z – most notably, the East African Safari rally, the world's most gruelling sports car event. In 1971, the Datsun 240Z was the first vehicle to capture an overall victory in its first year of competition! This was followed by a fifth in 1972 and a win in 1973. In the 1972 Monte Carlo Rally, a 240Z (Number 5), driven by Rauno Aaltonen and Jean Todd came third overall, and ninth overall in 1973, driven by Tony Fall.

Car and Driver magazine named the 240Z as one of the ten best cars of the 1970s, and *Autocar* listed it in 26th place in its top 100 road tests, from the 5000 tests conducted since it started testing in 1928 – within the top 1 per cent of all cars.

The 240Z was built to be a light car, providing great performance and economy, but naivety in the process of rust protection meant that many cars went to the breaker's yard with body corrosion, but perfect mechanicals. It is for this reason I have included the specifications of cars from other countries. These are now imported in some numbers from the USA and Australia, as the climate, in some regions, was kinder to the bodies. Having a wider knowledge will be important if you are looking to buy into the Datsun 240Z world, and this book aims to help you buy one that's as good to drive as it is to look at.

Whether it's to restore, modify, or simply use as an everyday classic, we hope you're rewarded with a Z that's exactly right for you. I have tried my best to ensure that the information in this book is correct to the best of my knowledge. However, whilst I refer to other models for context, this guide focuses only on the 240Z and the model that was originally destined for the UK.

A big 'thank you'

Although this book has an author's name on the cover, it couldn't have been achieved without the help of some key people. So, a big thank you to Karen France and Richard Wardle for their hospitality when I 'took over' their house for two whole days, going over every paragraph to ensure what I'd written was correct! Also to Mike Feeney of MJP Eastern Auto (see P58). Anyone who has been into Zs for any amount of time will have heard of Mike. He kindly supplied the list of OEM and pattern parts for the cost consideration section. Thanks also to Alan Thomas and Kats Endo. Alan is considered the foremost knowledge on S30s and Kats for providing an image of his beautiful Z432 (p61). But mostly, thank you to my wife, Sandy, for feeding and watering me, and her patience whilst we parked our camper van in the New Forest over numerous weekends to write this guide.

Contents

The Essential Buyer's Guide™ currency
At the time of publication a BG unit of currency "●" equals approximately £1.00/US$1.40/Euro1.14. Please adjust to suit current exchange rates using Sterling as the base currency.

The differences between a series 1 (left) and a series 2 (right) are subtle.

1 Is it the right car for you?

– marriage guidance

It might have the right lines, but is it right for you?

Old cars are narrow, and fit into the modern garage more readily than do modern cars!

Tall and short drivers
The Z is particularly spacious for two people, and the seats can accommodate drivers from 5ft 5in to 6ft 7in! The seats are thin, but support both passenger and driver well. The pedals are nicely offset, and are ideal for heel and toe operation.

Weight of controls
The steering is not power-assisted and the pedals are well modulated, but the throttle can be sticky due to the convoluted, direct linkage route from the pedal to the carburettors. The gear change is precise, but can be heavy when cold. All the dashboard controls work with the precision we now expect from a Japanese car.

Will it fit in the garage?
Wheelbase = 2305mm (90.7in)
Length = 4140mm (163.0in)
Width = 1626mm (64.0in)
Height = 1283mm (50.5in)

Interior space
Very spacious for driver and passenger. No rear seats, so only room for two.

Luggage capacity
The 240Z is a surprisingly practical sports car, especially as it has a large rear hatch to access the luggage area, with built-in straps to hold any loose items firmly in place. The spare wheel sits in a recess, below the luggage area, under the carpet.

Running costs
The body is lightweight (sub 1200kg) and the engine is lightly stressed so you can expect reasonable fuel economy: high 20s when cruising, and low 20s to high teens if you are driving it enthusiastically. The L24 engine is a simple SOHC engine, driven by a duplex timing chain. Servicing is very straightforward and everything is accessible. Service parts are still readily available, but some of the engine parts can be difficult to obtain.

Usability

One the 240Zs greatest attributes is its reliability, so cars racked up high mileages. Some owners use their car as a 'daily driver,' and it is capable, even now, of covering 20,000 miles a year without major issues.

Cars can be left in the garage (on a trickle charge) for weeks without creating any issues when it comes to starting. Just check the fluids first. There may be a delay whilst cranking, to wait for the pump to suck the fuel back through, but otherwise it starts first time.

Parts availability

Mechanical: Some parts are still available, however, with the passage of time, a lot of engine and gearbox internal components are now getting rare. Aftermarket replacement parts are slowly becoming available to replace OEM items. Body: Body parts are also becoming hard to find. Wings, doors, bonnets all unbolt, and secondhand panels are available from time to time, but can be expensive. The rear three-quarter panels are difficult to find and expensive.

An early rear three-quarter panel.

A late rear three-quarter panel – the badge includes the air vent.

Parts cost

Due to availability and demand the cost of parts can vary greatly. Some OEM parts can still be sourced via Nissan dealerships, but costs can be excessive and original part numbers will usually be required.

Insurance

Classic car insurance is available for the 240Z, and policies can be tailored to any car's specification, standard or modified. Reduced premiums can be given for mileage limitations and associated club membership. Note: any modifications should be declared before taking out any insurance policy.

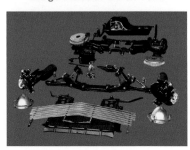

Service items, yes. Gearbox internals, no.

Investment potential

The 240Z was one of the first and most successful sports cars to come out of Japan and, as such, the investment potential is sound as desirability is high. Some halo models have fetched six figures, though models underneath this value can vary greatly. This is due, in part, to speculative selling.

Alternatives

Rivals to the 240Z ranged from the MGB/C and the Triumph Spitfire in the lower price brackets, through the Ford Capri 3.0 and Alfa Romeo GTV, to the Porsche 912, Mercedes SL and even the E-Type Jaguar in the upper price range.

2 Cost considerations
– affordable, or a money pit?

The purchase of a 240Z will always be a 'heart' decision, so beware: don't get caught up in the romance of these cars! The advice is always to buy the very best you can find and afford. A 10,000 car will cost more than 10,000 in restoration costs to make it a 20,000 car. Very good UK cars are now few and far between, so cars are being imported from the USA and Australia. This can be more affordable, but they may have suffered with cracked dashboards and sun-faded paint, so budget for the respray costs. The Samuri converted cars command higher prices, but make sure it is a real Samuri. There were reportedly only 74 made, and any list is not definitive. Rarer cars, such as the Z432 (PS30), have prices pushing six figures and are only available as an import from Japan, their home market.

Parts prices (P = Pattern, R = Refurbished.) Excluding VAT and shipping.

Panels
Sill (P) ●74.95
Wheelarch (P) ●79.95
Lower rear corner (P) ●97.50
Rear lower valence (P) ●165.00
Slam panel (P) ●97.50
Rear lower valence (P) ●165.00
Floorpan/chassis set (P) ●340.00
Front chassis repair set ●399.00
Suspension/Steering
Front lower ball joint ●39.95
Trackrod end ●27.95
Anti-roll bar drop link ●17.95 pr
Rear bush set (8 pc) ●136.40
KYB shocks (Front) ●119.95 pr
KYB shocks (Rear) ●109.95 pr
Urethane bush set ●199.95
Braking
Front pad set (P) ●21.95
Front disc (P) ●59.90 ea

Refurbished brake caliper (P)
●95.00 ea
Rear drums (P) ●228.85 pr
Engine
Felpro head set ●97.25
Conversion gasket set ●57.16
Conrod bearing set ●47.50
Main bearing set ●78.48
Carb gasket rebuild kit ●29.95
Cooling
Top hose ●26.09
Bottom hose ●28.24`
Heater hoses ●28.27 pr
Water pump ●41.50
Temp sender kit ●16.75
Interior (P)
Seat upholstery set (both)
●234.95
Carpet sets Front ●181.00
Quarter panel plastic trim ●89.95 ea

Electrical (P) (R)
Alternator ●95.00
Starter motor ●76.00
Voltage regulator ●26.95
General servicing (P)
Plug leads ●47.50
Distributor cap ●9.99
Rotor arm ●3.40
Air filter ●19.95
Oil filter (OEM) ●7.74
Fuel filter ●2.95
Contact points ●4.35
Miscellaneous
Harrington stainless bumper set
●750.00 apx
Fibreglass front valence/spoiler
●95.00
Lumenition electronic ignition (inc fit kit) ●176.00
Set of Wolfrace nuts (16) ●41.60

Secondhand parts prices
(Prices can vary enormously depending on availability and condition.) Excluding taxes and shipping.

Six branch performance exhaust ●400
Interior rear cargo three quarter trim ●150
Door card panels, left and right ●400
Clutch kit including pressure plate ●110
Complete glass rubber seal kit ●250

Complete carpet kit ●220
Front brake caliper upgrade kit - Toyota
●190
Silicone radiator coolant hose set ●250
Rear slam panel ●140

3 Living with a 240Z
– will you get along together?

The reputation of the Datsun 240Z in the sporting world is very high, with 240Zs being highly successful in both rallying and circuit motorsports. A 240Z Samuri entry even won its class in the 1974 BARC Blue Circle Modsport Championship, beating rival works competitors! There was only one HS30 model specification for UK supplied cars, so the choice is quite simple: select on condition and colour, in that order.

The 240Z is ideal as a daily car, although most are now coveted and are only shown on high days and dry days. Like most 1970s cars, the design of the electrical system had problems. Whilst far more reliable than British and European contemporaries, the fuse box and switches carried more current load than was ideal.

Depending on the type of use you want from your Z, there are a few modifications that make for a more reliable and pleasant ownership. An upgrade to the headlights is recommended. The standard bulbs were 45/55W, a simple upgrade is to either replace them with 80/100W bulbs together with a relay conversion, or LED replacements. These are 200% brighter and reduce the load on the fuse box.

With regard to the engine, the only real recommended change is to upgrade to electronic ignition. However, it does take away the therapeutic task of setting points. The engine has a pair of SU type carburettors, manufactured under licence by Hitachi, and once they are set correctly, they rarely go out of tune. The oil filter is readily to hand on the right-hand side of the engine, as is the dipstick. The engine, conveniently, takes exactly 5 litres of oil. The fuel filter is on the right inner wing, near the front of the engine bay, again, readily to hand.

The servo unit for the brakes is mounted on the bulkhead – in front of the servo is a tandem master cylinder with reservoirs that clearly display the fluid levels. To the left of this is the clutch master cylinder, providing very light clutch operation – again, the reservoir level is easy to view. At the back of the engine bay, there are two inspection panels that can only be lifted whilst the bonnet is open. On the left is the 12V negative earth battery, and on the right is the windscreen washer bottle, with the pump located directly underneath. This is opposite for LHD cars.

Service intervals were originally recommended every 3000 miles, which was common for Japanese cars. Most Zs probably don't cover more than 3000 miles a year nowadays anyway.

The interior is predominantly PVC and is hard wearing, but it was an area where Nissan saved on cost. Seatbelts are static in the early models, but were upgraded to inertia reels on later models. UK-supplied cars had seatbelts fitted in the UK by Britax. The window winding mechanism is manual. The driving position is very comfortable, and the dished steering wheel falls readily to hand. The thin indicator stalk

Do you want to go racing?

is on the right, and has the headlamp flasher button on the end. The stalk also alternates between dipped and main beam if you pull it towards you.

On the left of the steering column is a multi stalk switch, the 240Z being one of the first cars to have one. As such, it works quite well; the drum closest to the steering wheel has a lever on it to operate the sidelights and headlights. The drum on the outside operates the wipers. The early models had just two speeds, with the later models (from July 1972 onwards) incorporating an intermittent wipe.

Do you want it for the road?

On the end of the stalk is a button for the windscreen washer. Up until June 1972, the hazard lights switch set into the dash was an option.

In front of the driver are two dials, deeply recessed in cowls. These house the rev counter and speedometer. In the centre of the dashboard are three more dials, comprising the clock, ammeter, fuel, temperature and oil pressure gauges. Below these are three heater control levers: the upper one for heat or vent, the central for temperature control, and the lower for defrost or 'room.'

Do you want to go rallying?

Values are variable, depending on age, history and condition.

A rotary knob, to the left of these three levers, controls the three-speed fan motor. Very few cars still have the original optional radio.

Due to the lack of a voltmeter and charging warning light, there is little indication on the 240Z that the battery is discharging.

The glovebox, which is quite shallow, is opened via a lockable push button, and behind each seat are two more storage areas, set vertically with plastic covers on the early models and incorporated into the luggage bay on the later versions.

In the luggage bay, there are two tall turrets where the top of the rear suspension is mounted, but otherwise the area is quite cavernous.

The rear lights are accessed from the luggage area through two inspection panels that can be unscrewed to change bulbs.

Driving a 240Z is as easy as driving any other Datsun. All the controls are faithful, and there is a very comfortable left foot rest next to the clutch pedal. The engine is noisy from the cabin, but that is part of the attraction as the straight six sings beautifully. The gear change is a little mushy and slow, but gets better once the gearbox is warm. There is no anti-dive in the suspension, and the handling is typically 'slow in, fast out.'

The inspection panels are handy to gain access for charging.

Access to components is excellent.

The 240Z loves to run regularly and has no problem covering huge mileages in a day, with stories of 500-mile runs commonplace. The temperature sits just above the centre line, and the oil pressure, although it drops at idle, sits at around 60psi when cruising.

Once sorted, a 240Z is really easy to live with. They are a classic car that you work on because you want to, not because you have to. It's not until you go to a classic car show that you realise how many people the 240Z has touched; it might just have been a ride in a friend's car, or the person owned one for a time. Either way, everyone regrets selling theirs. It's a car that definitely gets under your skin!

A Samuri will certainly stand out.

www.velocebooks.com / www.veloce.co.uk
Details of all current books • New book news • Special offers • Gift vouchers • Forum

11

4 Relative values
– which model for you?

Some auction sites show 240Zs for sale for over ●50k, but for anything other than famous, unique, historic or ultra low-mileage examples, the prices can vary considerably. Whilst there was only one model specification imported to the UK, other types of HS30 have been personally imported, the majority from the USA. One of the reasons for the variation in prices, which isn't peculiar to the 240Z, is the increasing amount of cars that are registered in the UK.

In 1997, the DVLA listed just 81 examples left in the UK – by 2017, that figure had steadily risen to 203 examples, but over half are listed as SORN. As a guide, the earlier the model, the more desirable/valuable it is, and the better the investment. However, there is a good argument for preferring the later, better developed models. Because of scarcity, the early examples will command higher prices generally.

Any model made in small numbers has the potential to be coveted, sought after and valued. Nissan manufactured 420 Fairlady Z432s (PS30) for the domestic market, and, although rumours abound, one is yet to appear in public in the UK. There were two specifications of the PS30: the Z432 and the lightweight Z432R. Consequently these command stratospheric, six-figure plus prices compared to the standard S30 versions, but they appear undervalued when compared to the seven figures demanded for the Toyota 2000GT, of which 351 were produced.

In the UK, the Samuri was a standard 240Z modified by Race Head Services for fast road or race competition. It produced approximately 74 examples. The upgrades made the cars very effective on the track, and extremely quick for the road. They were easily identifiable due to their striking '70s colours scheme of orange and bronze. The Samuris are deemed by some to be more valuable than the standard car, although the listing or register of converted cars is approximate, and identification is reliant on the founder of the business.

With so few early UK 240Zs remaining, they are difficult to value, but a standard car in good to excellent condition can command values between ●25k and ●50k. Unless the mileage/usage is extremely low, the emphasis regarding price is on condition and originality. There are many examples still running well with mileages in excess of 250,000 miles.

Values – a rough guide, based on equality of condition.

Year	RHD*	Samuri**	LHD***
1973	£25K	£35K	£15K
1972	>+10%	>+15%	>+20%
1971	>+30%	>+30%	>+40%
1970	>+60%	>+50%	>+60%
1969	>+100%	>+70%	>+80%

* Standard HS30) – ** Samuri with provenance – *** Standard HLS30

5 Before you view
– be well informed

Knowledge is power, so do your homework. The 'Achilles heel' for most cars from the 1970s is rust. Protection was in its infancy and Japanese cars were affected more than most. It was assumed that because Japan doesn't use salt on its roads the manufacturer didn't understand the issues of corrosion, which only came to the fore when it began building light monocoque cars. The truth, however, was actually to do with the weight classification in the USA. Nissan wanted the 240Z to be under the 2300lb classification in that market, and adding an anti-rust treatment in the factory would have tipped the scales, so Nissan requested that the dealers provide the treatment prior to sale. Unfortunately, most dealers didn't carry out this request, so it was easy for the rust to take hold. In conclusion, anywhere there is metal, there could be rust – the usual areas of inner wings, crossmembers, chassis legs, sills and bulkheads are obvious areas to check.

Where is the car?
If the car is a good distance away, try to get as much information as possible (including images) before you embark on your journey, especially if you are looking to import a car. A personal import may appear to be a good route to take, but ensure that the car in question has resided in a 'dry climate' for most of its life. A 240Z that has been in the northern states of the US will fare little better than a UK car, but a genuine Californian car, still used as a daily driver, can be a good investment. Be aware though, that sun can damage the car as well as salt. If the car has been left outside, sunlight will deteriorate the dashboard over time, and other interior pieces will dry out and crack. Interior items can be tricky to find. Also ask how it is going to be shipped. There have been many horror stories of clean and straight cars arriving damaged after being shipped. It's not unheard of, for example, for people to walk over a car to get to another item at the back of a shipping container. Don't forget to add the shipping cost and import taxes to your budget, which are likely to be significant.

A close inspection is a must.

Dealer or private sale

It's important to establish whether the seller is a private individual or a dealer. There are many importers in the marketplace, but it's important to know who you are dealing with. A private owner is likely to know far more detail and history of any car offered for sale than a dealer is.

Be very careful if you are buying a vehicle of note, such as a Samuri. Use a relevant owners' club – that's what they are there for – and make sure the chassis and engine numbers tie up with the relevant paperwork and manufacturer's information. If the dealer is offering a warranty, make sure you get that in writing, and understand what is and isn't covered.

There are some cars that have been converted from left- to right-hand drive – this is perfectly acceptable if done correctly, and the seller shouldn't hide this. For example, if you find a RHD 240Z with sidelights on the rear quarter or the chassis identity plate on the left hand B-pillar (these were only put on cars destined for the USA) then it has been converted (or it's had a US rear three-quarter fitted), but these are reasons to ask questions. The chassis should say HLS30, the 'L' denoting LHD.

Cost of collection or delivery

A dealer may be able to quote a price including delivery, and arrange transportation, but sometimes it can be as important to see the premises as well as the car. This is especially pertinent for a private sale. If you view the car at the seller's address, you can confirm the address on the log book, it's just another tick on your checklist. (Do have a checklist, because buying a 240Z can be an emotional experience.)

View – when and where

If you have the opportunity to see from underneath the car, take it, as these cars rust from the inside out. There are many shiny cars on top, but information gained from viewing underneath can tell you more about the history of a car than anything else.

If it is a business they should have the facilities to provide this, if it's a private sale make sure you bring a trolley jack and some overalls. You can safely jack up the car on the differential at the back, and on the engine mounting crossmember. Don't use the jacking points recommended by the manufacturer, as they were never the best, even when new. Make sure you safely place axle stands before crawling underneath.

Always view the car outside, preferably in bright sunlight, as that will show up any shortcomings. Although there are some great photographs of cars taken at night and in the wet, that is not the time to view or buy one.

Reason for sale?

Datsun 240Zs have a tendency to get under the owner's skin – the more they drive it, the more they love it, and almost without exception people do regret selling theirs. So, if someone is selling their beloved car, find out why. Many ownerships stretch to 20, 30 or even 40 years, so given this, there must be a good reason to sell, and, if there is, that could make it a good reason to buy.

Multiple owners are not necessarily a bad thing. After all, you are looking at a car that is half a century old. Information like old MoTs can be a great source of enlightenment about the car in front of you. Cross check the registration on the DVLA website, check-mot.service.gov.uk. If a car has been laid up for any time then the mileage recorded should reflect that. If a car has a history of failing every year, then passing, this may indicate that just enough work is being done to keep it on the road, not congruent with tender loving care. You can also check the advisory information on each test. But if the reason is acceptable and believable, you could be in the right place at the right time.

Left-hand drive to right-hand drive
As mentioned before, there is no issue if the work is carried out correctly. In fact, conversion components for the bodyshell are now available on-line. The issue is if the work is being done to hide an identity, or to present a Z as something it is not. More than half of all 240Zs that are now in the UK are LHD – many owners have restored their beloved UK car using components from a US donor, as it is cheaper and quicker than trying to restore an excessively corroded bodyshell. The seller should celebrate that their car has been restored and share that story with you. If they don't, be guarded.

Condition (body/chassis/interior/mechanicals)
A 240Z is all about condition. Panel gap consistency was never that great on any '70s car, but panels should line up. A magnet can be your best friend. Chapter 7 will delve into this in more detail.

All original specification
Many 240Zs suffered at the hands of back street bodgers. 30 years ago they could have bought a 240Z for a few hundred pounds, and many had engine transplants, the Buick V8 engine from Rover being the favourite. As the Z became more revered, the ones that were left began being restored to original condition and, as with other cars, it is the original specification models that are now attracting the most money.

As the price goes up, details regarding the original specification become more important. An original spec 240Z with historic provenance is the most valuable.

Match data/legal ownership
Do VIN/chassis, engine numbers and licence plate match the official registration document? Is the owner's name and address recorded in the official registration documents?

For those countries that require an annual test of roadworthiness, (an MoT certificate in the UK, which can be verified online at www.gov.uk/check-mot-status or by calling 0845 600 5977). Does the car have a document showing that it complies?

If a smog/emissions certificate is mandatory, does the car have one?

If required, does the car carry a current road fund licence/licence plate tag?

Does the vendor own the car outright? Money might be owed to a finance company or bank: the car could even be stolen. Several organisations will supply the data on ownership, based on the car's licence plate number, for a fee.

Such companies can often also tell you whether the car has been 'written-off' or has a salvage title, sometimes sellers list a written-off car as a Cat C/D or on 'VCar.'

A category C or D car represents an uneconomic insurance write-off. These can be a cost effective way of buying a car, but they are harder to sell on, and you need to check the quality of repairs very carefully. In the UK, these organisations can supply vehicle data.

- HPI – 01722 422 422
- AA – 0870 600 0836
- DVLA – 0870 240 0010
- RAC – 0870 533 3660
- Other countries will have similar organisations.

Unleaded fuel

Although originally designed for leaded fuel only, the L24 straight six engine will happily run on unleaded without any modification, although filling up with a premium (98+ octane) brand every fourth time is recommended, as is a lead replacement additive. If your engine is tuned, use a higher octane fuel and additives all the time.

Insurance

Always ensure you are covered before driving any prospective purchase.

How can you pay?

A cheque/check will take several days to clear and the vendor may prefer to sell to a cash buyer. However a banker's draft (a cheque issued by a bank) is as good as cash, but safer, so contact your own bank and become familiar with the formalities that are necessary to obtain one.

Buying at an auction

If the intention is to buy at auction, see chapter 10 for further advice.

Professional vehicle check (mechanical examination)

The are often marque/mode specialists who will undertake professional examination of a vehicle on your behalf. Owners' clubs will be able to put you in touch with such organisations. Other organisations that will carry out a general professional check in the UK are:

- AA – 0800 085 3007
- ABS – 0800 358 5855
- RAC – 0870 533 3660

www.velocebooks.com / www.veloce.co.uk
Details of all current books • New book news • Special offers • Gift vouchers • Forum

16

6 Inspection equipment
– these items will really help

This book
Reading glasses (if you need them for close up work)
Magnet, a fridge magnet will do
Torch
A probe (a small screwdriver will suffice)
Overalls
An inspection mirror or borescope
Camera or smartphone
A friend, preferably a knowledgeable enthusiast

Buying a classic car is an exciting and emotional experience, but gather yourself first. As they say, luck is merely preparation crossed with opportunity, so let's prepare to be lucky. Gather a few items that will help as you work your way around the car. This book is designed to be your guide at every step, so take it along and use the check boxes in Chapter 9 to help you assess each area of the car. Don't be afraid to let the seller see you using it.

Take your reading glasses if you need them to read documents and make close up inspections.

A magnet will help you check if the car has filler, or fibreglass panels. Use the magnet to sample body panels, but be careful not to damage the paintwork. Expect to find a little filler here and there, but not over extensive areas. There's

nothing wrong with fibreglass panels, but a purist might want the car as originally built.

A torch with fresh batteries will be useful for peering into wheelarches and under the car.

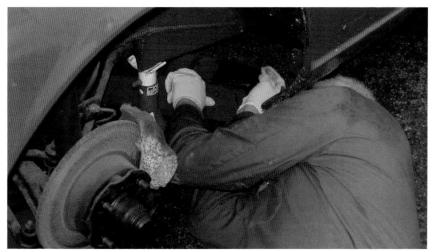

Be prepared to get down 'n' dirty!

A small probe, maybe a screwdriver, can be used – with care – particularly in the wheelarches and on the underside. With this you should be able to check areas of suspect corrosion, but be cautious – if it's really bad the probe might go right through the metal!

Be prepared to get dirty. Take along a pair of overalls if you have them. A variable angle inspection mirror will help you check inaccessible areas you can't normally get to. A borescope is cheap enough now and this would even allow you to view inside the cylinder bores, inside the sills, or even the chassis rails!

If you have a digital camera, or a good quality smartphone, take it along so that you can study some areas in more detail later. Take a picture of any part of the car that causes you concern, and seek a friend's opinion

Ideally, have a friend or knowledgeable enthusiast to accompany you: a second opinion is always valuable and they will tell you to walk away or bite the sellers arm off – especially if the car you're viewing is a rare or sought after model with supposed history.

7 Fifteen minute evaluation
– walk away or stay?

General condition

Any Datsun is renowned for its reliability, and the 240Z is no different. Because they are so easy to maintain, any car with an MoT should have an engine that runs sweetly, a gearbox that is positive, and a differential which may be a bit clunky, but otherwise is in good order.

There are always two sides to evaluating a car: the mechanical side, and the body side. With the 240Z, the focus should always be on the body. For reasons explained previously, Nissan didn't underseal the cars because of weight taxation rules in the USA – instead, it trusted the dealers to apply any anti-rust treatment, but as we know, a dealer is always focused on the next sale, so the treatment wasn't applied by most dealerships. Consequently, 240Zs rusted ... a lot!

It's a simple monocoque design.

Unmolested cars are easier to evaluate than modified ones. Apart from the value aspect, it also intimates that the model you are looking at is less likely to have been abused than one that has spent many a night in someone's garage and been at the mercy of a welder's torch.

Look at the car from 20 feet away to see whether it 'sits right.' They originally had quite a gap between the top of the tyre and the arch, so, if one has been lowered, the first question to ask is has it been lowered properly, or has a ring been lopped off of one of the coils? The 240Z is a beautiful car, and it is easy to 'fall' for the first car you see (I did!), so try and keep an objective mind. That way love won't turn into heartache.

The 'trumpets' under the wing can suffer badly from rust.

Body

On the plus side, the headlamp cowls, lower front valances (left, right and middle), bonnet, front wings, scuttle panel, doors and tailgate are all bolt-on items – on the negative side, ensure that any replacement panel has the metal and captive nuts to attach it!

Underneath, and running the length of each front inner wing, are reinforcing panels, commonly called 'trumpets.' As well as strengthening, these supply a ram airflow for footwell ventilation, from just inside the front of the engine bay to outlets below the dashboard. The panels are a metal pressing, which form a dirt trap in the wheelarch, between the top of the panel and the underside of the wing. This means that by the time any rust appears on the top of wing, it's likely that the trumpet has rotted through. Moving further back, the sills on each side will need good use of your magnet to ensure all is well. Keep it handy for the bottom of the doors and check the drain holes on the underside of each door, as water collected in the bottom of the door has nowhere to go if these are blocked.

Rear wheelarch repairs panels are available. If fitted, it was always difficult to recreate the subtle crease that flows along the side of the car directly above the rear wheel, so check for a crease. Look at the back of the car, check the tailgate, especially at the bottom as it suffers the same fate as the doors, plus the 'slam panel,' which forms the lower part of the tailgate aperture, particularly where it joins the rear three-quarter panel.

Chassis

Although of monocoque design, the chassis rail elements are simple in concept. Two longitudinal 'legs' start at a radiator crossmember and run along the bottom of each side of the engine bay, continuing under the floorpan, and finishing just behind the seats. The floorpans connect the chassis rails to the inner sills and transmission

tunnel. A secondary pair of chassis legs reinforces the rear floor assembly, and are shaped to provide room for the independent rear suspension, spare wheel well and the fuel tank. The rear rails terminate at the final rear crossmember. Due to the lack of panel seam sealing, check anywhere two panels have been welded together. The chassis legs themselves are prone to the bug, and there are many floorplans that resemble those in Fred Flintstone's mode of transport!

A well cared-for engine bay will tell a story.

Because almost any area of the bodyshell can rust, it's virtually impossible to just cut away one component without having to repair or make good corrosion in the panel it was welded to. Condition is everything.

An undersealed body can be a double-edged sword: on the one hand the chassis has been protected from rusting further, but on the other it could be there just to hide all sorts of gremlins underneath. So your probe could come in quite handy.

Underbonnet

The condition of the inner wings is a good sign of the overall condition of a 240Z. Check at the bottom of the inner wing, where it attaches to the chassis leg, and the lower reinforcement panel of the front suspension strut – this is where the rot can start to take hold. Checking it from the engine bay side and under the arch will give you the evidence. The scuttle panel in front of the windscreen has slats to allow airflow to the heater fan, and for the window washer jets. Unfortunately, they also allow water and dirt to accumulate in the cavity below. There are drains at in each corner, but these can get blocked, leading to corrosion of the bulkhead welded joints. Anywhere there is a battery, there is the probability of rust. The tray sits on the opposite side of the driver.

The engine should be oil tight, except for the sump gasket area, which can leak a little, but this is nothing be alarmed about. The car is also normally watertight, so check the hoses and the water pump, which sits behind the fan.

Test drive

Any Datsun normally starts instantly, and the 240Z should be no different. If it's cold it will need a little choke, if it's warm just turn the key. One thing to note is when you turn the key to the 'ignition on' position a red light will appear at the bottom of the speedometer – many people mistake this for the ignition light. The 240Z does not have an ignition light! This is a handbrake warning light, which of course goes off when you release the handbrake. The later models, 260Z onwards, fixed this by replacing the ammeter with a voltmeter and a red charge warning light.

DATSUN	TYPE	H S 3 0
ENGINE CAPACITY	2 3 9 3	c c
MAX. HP at RPM	150HP/6000RPM	SAI
WHEEL BASE	2 3 0 5	mm
ENGINE NO.	L 24 – 0 7	
CAR NO.	H S 3 0 – 0	

NISSAN MOTOR CO., LTD.
YOKOHAMA JAPAN

One of the rare places where Datsun and Nissan are printed together.

The clutch is hydraulically operated and should be light in operation. If it is a standard clutch the take-up should be smooth. Engine control is of a direct linkage design from the accelerator pedal to the carburettors, utilising a series of rods and pivots, not a cable. If it's not maintained correctly it can make the throttle operation somewhat jerky. If you do experience this, it is likely to be the linkage, not the carbs.

The gearbox is direct but heavy, with a long throw when compared to modern examples. The four-speed is a standard H pattern with reverse 'to the right and back.' The five-speed is similar, but with fifth gear 'to the right and away.'

The car should pull away smoothly and be easy to drive; not intimidating at all. Although the engine is a short stroke design it can be a bit breathless above 5000rpm, even though the redline is not until 6500rpm. I think this just shows Nissan's confidence in the engine. As the gearbox warms up, the gear change will become easier and lighter, although will still be a bit slow. The engine should warm quickly, and the temperature gauge should read approximately halfway when the car is in normal operating range.

The standard brakes should be easy to modulate, but will need a firm push to bring the car to a halt. Most owners agree that the brakes are a little under spec and a number of cars have modified brake systems.

Being front-engined and rear-wheel drive, cornering will be the traditional 'slow in' and 'fast out' approach.

This is the handbrake light, not the ignition light.

Zs love to be driven, so a test drive should leave you with a smile on your face.

The steering is heavy at low speeds, more so if it has aftermarket wheels, but does lighten up nicely at speed. It weighs down again when cornering, and although the car will lean in a corner it is quite well contained. There may be a little slack around the straight ahead, but being rack and pinion it should be direct and easy to place.

The engine should pull cleanly from almost any revs. Aftermarket electronic ignition can make a major difference to the driveability, particularly at low and high rpm. The engine sound is wonderful! Listen for clonks in the suspension and drivetrain – vibration may be due to any one of the six universal joints in the driveshafts, from the back of the gearbox through to the rear wheels. Noises could be due to worn suspensions joints, but could also be evidence of accident damage or corrosion.

Interior

The interior of a 240Z is a sober affair, with lots of black. Although there were other options, the black interior was by far the most popular. Of course, now it means if you come across a coloured interior, especially if it's a white car with a peacock blue interior, its rarity may add value.

The seats are thin but supportive and covered in PVC plastic – cold in the winter, hot in the summer! Two versions of the seats are available, one with limited backrest adjustment by way of a knob, the other with a lever to provide a fold forward and recline operation.

In front of the driver is a three-spoke steering wheel with a resin finished wood-like effect contoured rim – it is quite thin, and not to everyone's tastes. Behind the steering wheel are two recessed cowls, on the left is the rev counter complete with the indicator direction lights at the bottom, and on the right is the speedo, odometer and resettable trip meter, with the handbrake warning light at the bottom and the high beam light at the top.

In the middle of the dashboard, are three cowls, housing five gauges. Below these instruments is a map-reading light with the heater controls underneath. If there is a radio it will be fitted at the bottom centre of the dashboard, where it meets the centre console.

The centre console houses the ashtray, choke mechanism, heated rear window switch and fuse box.

The interior door cards are covered in padded PVC, and in the rear luggage area are moulded panels, which are unique for left and right. If these have been cut or altered, which was often the case when extra speakers were required, be aware that replacements can be hard to find.

Carpets for the front footwells and hatch area are simply laid in place, and therefore can easily be lifted to check to rot and water ingress.

Modifications

Whilst it's cheaper to buy a car that is already modified than to buy a standard one and modify it yourself, there are a couple of downsides. One, the car will never be to the specification you had in your head, and two, modifications can hide an array of substandard work, all of which will have to be corrected for your own peace of mind.

The vents in the backrest are not real.

Peacock blue is *the* valuable interior.

Factory modified 240Zs are extremely rare, so when one comes up for sale, it should be a straightforward process – use one of the clubs to determine if it is legitimate or not.

The Samuris have been accepted by many circles in the UK (but not all) as an acknowledged modification. The problem is there is no definitive register of the 74 cars that are supposed to have been built. Note: Samuri cars were never sanctioned by Nissan.

Most owners modify their 240Zs to add their own 'signature.' Depending on what type of car you are looking for, if the modifications can be simply unbolted then it is worth considering.

Braking modifications can be made by using Toyota four-pot or even Range Rover calipers. There is also a rear disc conversion available.

Unless they have been welded in, aftermarket seats can easily be unbolted and standard ones fitted.

A lot of cars are now starting to get LED upgrades. These make sense for two reasons: one, they are brighter and therefore safer, and two, they reduce the load through the fuse box and switchgear, which is always a good thing.

Because of the basic competency of the suspension, which keeps the wheel perpendicular to the road, fitting bigger wheels improves the handling, but it can make the steering unacceptably heavy. Make sure they don't foul the arches, and if they don't, check that someone hasn't merely folded the arch lip back on itself.

Identification

The Vehicle Identification Number (VIN) for all HS30 models can be found in two places. The first and primary place is stamped at the factory into the upper engine bulkhead panel on the right-hand side. The second stamping can be found on a photo-etched aluminium VIN plate located on the right-hand side inner wing. US models also have the VIN etched on a plate and set into the dashboard, visible through the windscreen and on an additional build data plate located on the B pillar of the driver's side door.

• S30 – Basic Nissan Fairlady Z fitted with an L20 engine
• PS30 – Nissan Fairlady Z8 432 fitted with an S20 engine (4 valves, 3 carburettors, 2 camshafts)
• PS30-SB – Nissan Fairlady Z 432R fitted with an S20 engine and specifically built for racing purposes
• HS30 – Basic Datsun 240Z/Nissan Fairlady 240Z fitted with an L24 engine.
• HLS30 – left-hand drive

The most popular mod at the time was the ubiquitous Wolfrace wheel.

- HLS30-U – North American market
- HS30-L – Upgraded version fitted with five-speed gearbox and other luxuries
- HS30-A – Fitted with automatic gearbox
- HS30-U – Right-hand drive
- HS30-V – Fitted with emission control device
- HS30-Q – Destined for Europe
- HS30-M – Destined for Australia
- HS30-H(G) – Nissan Fairlady 240ZG fitted with an L24 engine and 'Gnose' aerodynamic package which included headlight covers and fender flares

Chassis suffixes 'L,' 'A,' 'U,' 'Q,' V,' 'M,' 'SB' and 'H' were not found on the chassis itself, but rather were used by the factory to reference particular models.

Unfortunately, the cars were not completed in chassis serial number sequence, ie they did not roll off a single assembly line in serial number order. Nissan used one serial number set for the HLS30 chassis, and another serial number set for the HS30 chassis. It is quite possible you will find a car with the same serial, but with a different prefix. Approximately 4000 RHD (HS30) 240Zs were produced between 1969 and the end of the 1972 model year. Then in both the HS and HLS serial number sequence, Nissan jumped ahead to restart the serial numbers for the 1973 model year. The HLS30 series restarted at HLS30 120xxx, and the HS serial numbers restarted at HS30 100xxx.

Type	(X) (X) S30
Engine capacity	XXXXcc
Max HP at RPM	XXXHP/XXXX RPM (SAE)
Wheelbase	2305mm
Engine number	LXX - XXXXXX (stamped)
Car number	(X) (X) S30 XXXXXX (stamped)

Some cars just look 'right.'

8 Key points

– where to look for problems

Rusted is busted

There is a uncorroborated story that a number of 240Zs were delayed at a UK dock on arrival because of an administrative error. While the cars remained there, they fell victim to a large storm, and legend has it that these cars sat in seawater for two weeks.

A Z can rust anywhere.

Check anywhere there are welds – always a starting point for rust.

Any car subjected to that would not survive long, but even disregarding this story, 240Zs did rust badly, and often cars under five years old were failing MoTs due to corrosion. Ironically, English-manufactured cars fared better because an engine leak sprayed a fine mist of oil over the underside of the chassis, which provided an almost perfect resistance to rust. The Japanese oil-tight engines only exacerbated the problem, and rust appeared within months of cars being registered.

Check anywhere and everywhere for corrosion. If you are able to check inside box sections using a borescope (they're not expensive), so much the better. Wings, trumpets, doors, hatch, outer sills, inner sills, floor pans, chassis legs: check them all! Even the bumpers weren't chromed to UK standard – the original application was very thin, and lacked weather-resistance.

Underbonnet

Look for signs of rot on the inner wings, bulkhead and battery tray, and check the chassis legs all the way along, especially where the front anti-roll bar mounts. Many cars have matching engine and chassis numbers. The Z doesn't, but the VIN plate does list the engine number, so it's worth checking against the number stamped on the engine cylinder block. This is located on the right (oil filter side) of the engine, right at the back, close to the cylinder head. Check for emulsion under the oil filler cap, and for water leaks near the head gasket and around the thermostat and housing. If the thermostat hasn't been changed for years, it's likely that the bolts will shear. Check hoses for damage and leaks and any damage to the radiator.

A spacious interior for two people.

Interior and trim

Zs imported from hotter climates have the advantage of an intact body, but may have succumbed to splits in the dashboard where the hot weather has dried out the resin in the plastic. Replacement dashboards can be expensive to buy, and a significant effort to fit. Original carpet sets are not available, but many companies will provide good quality replacements (better than original in fact), but the plastic trim is now very hard to find, and expensive when you do. Returning a modified 240Z interior to standard can end up costing thousands.

9 Serious evaluation
– 60 minutes for years of enjoyment

Circle Excellent (4), Good (3), Average (2) or Poor (1) for each check, and add up points at the end. Any evaluation check must be realistic. Sole responsibility lies with the buyer to be vigilant and not to cut corners over the next 60 minutes. Take it seriously, get it right, and you will be able to make an informed decision on whether to purchase. Get it wrong, and it could become your worst nightmare.

Engine   [4] [3] [2] [1]

The majority of 240Zs have the original L-series engine, with the L24's 2393cc capacity (2.4-litre, hence the name 240Z). The L-series of engines was produced from 1967 to 1986 in both four- and six-cylinder configurations, with engine capacity ranging from 1300cc to 2800cc. The four-cylinder variant was also the engine used for the dependable Datsun 510. The L-series engine is known for its extreme reliability, durability, and parts interchangeability. It's a two-valve per cylinder, SOHC, non-crossflow design, with cast iron block and an aluminium cylinder head. The twin carburettors for the HS30 were made, under license, by Hitachi, and are based on the Skinners Union (SU) design. Parts are not, however, interchangeable with standard SU carburettors.

Engine is big and heavy, though simple in design.

The head ID can be found between plugs 1 and 2 on the right-hand side.

The engine is believed to be derived from the four-cylinder design by Mercedes-Benz, which was licensed to Prince Motor Company. By the time Prince was absorbed by Nissan in 1966, it had altered the design to the point that it no longer required licensing. The engine still resembles a Mercedes in many ways, particularly the valve train. With a full duplex timing chain, there is no danger of a snapped timing belt, but just because they don't break doesn't mean they can't stretch, so don't forget to check and adjust it!

The engine is capable of stellar mileage, if oil changes are completed regularly.

No expansion tank – what you see is what you get.

The L-series is pretty bullet-proof as we know, and problems usually arise only through lack of maintenance, like silting up of the water passages at the rear of the cylinder block which can cause overheating – this can also lead to corrosion of the rear core plug.

Leaking head gaskets and associated anti-freeze damage to the coolant passages in the head is another problem that can arise, and the early metal cooling fans can cause premature wear to the coolant pump. The distributor rotor shaft bushes can wear after a while, causing the rotor spindle to move laterally, making it impossible to get a consistent points gap, but this can be remedied by having phosphor bronze bushes made by any precision-engineering firm.

Cylinder heads

The 240Z does have a couple of components that affect the performance and value of the car, namely two types of cylinder head. I have listed all of the heads from the later and larger capacity series for completeness, as the one you're looking at may have a later block/head combination.

Head type	Production years	Compression ratio	Description
E31 Part # 11041-E3100	1969-71 (240Z)	9.13:1	An uncommon and desirable head. Its chambers were high-quench designs, however, the valves were smaller than the 260 and 280 heads. E31s are rare, and use an external oil spray bar.
E88 Part # 11041-E8800 & 11041-E8801	09/71-05/72 06/72-07/73 (240Z)	(240Z) 8.8:1	The E88 came on the 1971-73 240s. It had a lower compression and used an external oil spray bar.
N35 Part #11041-N3500	08/73 (260Z)	(260Z) 8.26:1	Similar to the E88 but with larger valves. It uses an external oil spray bar.
N42	1975-76 (280Z)	8.29:1	The larger valve N42 came on the 1975-76 280Z. The head came with softer brass valve seats for use with leaded gas. It uses an external oil spray bar.
N47	1977-80 (280ZX)	8.29:1	The N47 has diamond-shaped exhaust ports with emission liners. Fitted with steel valve seats for use with unleaded gas. It uses internal lubrication (oil holes in cam lobes).
P79	1981-83 (280ZX)	8.82:1	The P79 came with flat-top pistons on the L28- F54 blocks. The exhaust ports/liners are identical to the N47, and it uses an internally oiled cam.
P90	1981-82 (280ZX Turbo)	7.38:1	This is the turbo head from the '81-82 ZX. It has the same combustion chambers as the P79, but has square exhaust ports like the N42. It uses an internally oiled cam.
P90a	1981-82 (280ZX Turbo)	7.38:1	Like the P90, but it has hydraulic valve lifters. It has identical chambers and ports to the P90, and uses an internally oiled cam.

Carburettors

Carburettors fitted to the L24 engine differed throughout the 240Z's production, as emission regulations grew ever more stringent in the JDM and various export markets. European specification models were equipped with twin Hitachi SU type, side-draught carburettors, of two basic specifications. From 1969 until August 1971, the Hitachi HJG46W-3A (or -4 for automatic transmission) were fitted. This type of carburettor is easily identified from the four screws that secure the dashpot to the throttle body. From September 1971 to July 1973, a revised design was incorporated, which has only three screws securing the dashpot.

The intakes for the 1970-71 carbs are the same, but the balance tube was assembled with different fittings, while the 1972 intake was water-warmed to help atomize the fuel faster when the engine was cold, with changes in the heat shield between the carbs and the exhaust manifold. There is little difference in the performance of each type of carb, but this may be important for identification.

In the US, from June 1972, a completely new design of carburettor was introduced. Hitachi HMB46Ws were known as 'flat-tops,' due to the revised dashpot design. Although these met the current emission regulations, they made the car undriveable. This was replaced by a fuel-injection system upon introduction of the 280Z in 1976. If you find a car with this setup, it is recommended that you remove and replace with either variant of the HJG46W carburettors.

Air cleaners

The original air cleaner is quite large, as it is a single unit that filters the air for both carbs. Originally in orange for the HJG46W-style carburettors, and blue for the HMB46W-style, some have been replaced with aftermarket individual trumpet-like filters for each carb.

Air cleaners for cars destined for colder climates (including Europe) had an additional duct in the intake from the exhaust manifold, which acted as a heat riser to preheat incoming air during winter months. This was a manually-operated, spring-loaded flap valve, which could select either cold or warm air induction. Some imports may also have this feature.

Cooling system

The cooling system on the L24 engine was tested thoroughly in both cold and hot US climates before launch; it can, therefore, handle most situations with ease, but, as always, if it's not maintained, it can fail.

The most obvious cause of problems is when the mix of water and antifreeze is not correct. There is no expansion tank on a 240Z, so coolant level can be checked straight from the radiator cap. Discoloured water, especially red, indicates corrosion in the system, which blocks the radiator and heater matrix if not addressed.

If an otherwise standard engine has an additional fan, sometimes mounted in front of the original radiator, investigate whether this is being used to cover up overheating problems (although many owners do replace the original fan with an electric one, because you can gain up to 5bhp with this modification alone).

The coolant pump is mounted on the front engine casing, and drives a cooling fan via a viscous coupling. It normally gives trouble-free operation for many years, although, cars built before July 1971 may have a metal fan fitted – check for weeping, as the fan is quite heavy and unbalanced when compared to the later plastic fan. If you have a metal fan, don't panic; it only takes its toll on the water pump bearing after 15 to 20,000 miles. The thermostat is mounted on the top left side of the engine. Access is superb, but it can suffer the old issue of steel bolts screwed into aluminium heads. If they haven't been put in with something like copper slip, and/or have been left for a few years, you'll be lucky to get them out without them shearing off. The thermostat housing is a two-piece affair, which means it's not as much of an issue if a bolt breaks when trying to split the housing. If it's one of the bolts that screws into the head, the worst case scenario is having to have the head removed to remove the broken bolt. If this does happen, search for someone who specialises in removing sheared studs and bolts – it could save you a lot of time and money.

On the right-hand side of the engine, towards the back, the pipes change diameter before routing around the back of the cylinder head to warm the manifold, returning via the thermostat housing. This can also be a weak point. The originally fitted hose clips are dual wire design. Normal clips work just as well, but, as the values of these cars rise, having the correct clips becomes more important.

Exhaust systems

The standard mild steel exhaust was quite restrictive, and was installed by Nissan to keep down overall Noise Vibration and Harshness (NVH), as the rear suspension was perceived to be quite noisy. At the time it was a compromise, as the system lost the car a few 'horses.' It came with two silencers: one midway behind the gearbox, and the other part of a 'box 'n' tail' configuration.

Rear exhaust – great for packaging, not so good for protection from the rear wheel.

As the original exhaust is difficult to come by, most owners have installed a stainless steel system. The difference in performance is immediately noticeable with no apparent degradation in fuel economy, and, of course, it has a better sound.

Most leave the cast exhaust manifold in place. Replacing it can be fiddly, and some aftermarket manifolds don't fit well, but six into four into two tubular type 'headers' are available, which undoubtedly further improve the performance.

If the exhaust has a mild steel fitment, be aware that it might not last too long, even though the cars now tend to be driven longer distances, which gives the exhaust longer life, rather that the short, daily drives which never let the exhaust dry out properly.

The exhaust route follows the transmission and propshaft quite closely, and then routes up and over the rear suspension, with mounts before and after the suspension to hold it in place. Check the rear mounting to make sure it is in good condition, as it can receive a pounding from dirt thrown up by the nearside rear wheel.

Gearbox

Three transmission options were available for the 240Z. The basic model was offered with a four-speed manual, and the 240Z-L package was fitted with a five-speed manual. From April 1971 each model was offered with an optional 3N71B three-speed automatic gearbox. First-generation four- and five-speed gearboxes (Type A) were known as 'straight stick' types, and featured a three-piece gearbox casing with detachable bellhousing. The four-speed variant F4W71A was fitted to cars built up to August 1971, whilst the five-speed FS5C71A continued to be used until December 1971. The second generation four-speed and five-speed gearboxes (Type B) were known as 'bent stick' types, with the four-speed F4W71B applied to cars built after September 1971, until the five-speed FS5C71B was introduced in January 1972. The new design featured a new two-piece gearbox casing with integral bellhousing.

Manual gearbox

The four-speed box is lighter and was also cheaper – this allowed the 240Z to be sold below the required weight and desired price in the USA. Some markets also got the automatic as well, and, like most 1970s autos, it was nothing to write home about, but was deemed better than the usual slush boxes available. Autos are cheaper because the market wants manuals, but they can be converted to a manual.

Type	F4W71A <12/71	F4W71B >01/72	FS5C71A <12/71	FS5C71B >01/72
Speeds forward	4	4	5	5
Lubricant capacity	1.5 litres	1.5 litres	1.5 litres	1.5 litres
Gear ratios				
1st	3.549:1	3.592:1	2.957:1	2.906:1
2nd	2.197:1	2.246:1	1.857:1	1.902:1
3rd	1.420:1	1.415:1	1.311:1	1.308:1
4th	1.000:1	1.000:1	1.000:1	1.000:1
5th	–	–	0.852:1	0.864:1
Reverse	3.164:1	3.657:1	2.922:1	3.892:1
Speedometer ratio	17/6	17/6	19/6	19/6

Manual gearbox Identification

Gearbox ID	Option 1	Option 2	Option 3
Type of control	F = Floor	R = Remote	–
Transmission style	S = Special overdrive top gear	Blank = Direct drive top gear	
Number of forward speeds	3 = three-speed	4 = four-speed	5 = five-speed
Drive/synchro type	W = Warner type brass synchros	C = Steel Porsche style servo system	–
Gear spacing	Two digits = Distance between mainshaft and countershaft in mm		
Sequential model	A = first gen design	B = second gen design	–

For example; an early five-speed gearbox would have the ID 'FS5C71A.'

Automatic gearbox   4 3 2 1

The Jatco 3N71 transmission was the first three-speed automatic transmission from Nissan. It was introduced as a conventional alternative to the popular Borg-Warner Type 35. It was designed for use with a number of rear-wheel drive vehicles with longitudinal engines, including Mazda, Mercury and Ford.

Type	3N71B>04/71
Speeds forward	3
Lubricant capacity	5.5-litre
Gear ratios	
1st	2.458:1
2nd	1.458:1
3rd	1.000:
Reverse	2.182:1
Speedometer	unknown

The gear change should be smooth, and should change without any hesitancy. If it has problems, like not wanting to engage top gear, then start asking about when it last had an oil and filter change; this is normally the root of most problems, especially if it's been sitting for a couple of years. The seals can also become brittle and leak pressure. The pressure is required for proper shifting.

The gearlever falls readily to hand.

Clutch

All 240Zs have a hydraulically operated clutch system, with the master cylinder mounted on the bulkhead in the engine bay and the slave cylinder mounted on the right-hand side of the bell housing. It should be light in operation, and the pick up should be smooth. The clutch is a single dry-disc diaphragm spring type. Judder or slip, points to a worn clutch plate, or oil leaking from the rear crankshaft bearing.

A simple clutch master cylinder.

Propshaft

There were two basic types of propshaft used on the 240Z, both variations having a universal joint (UJ) at each end. The first type, sometimes known as the 'two-piece propshaft,' was used in conjunction with the original five-speed manual gearbox (FS5C71A). The design featured the sliding portion, lubricated by grease, as an integral part of the propshaft, and a four-bolt locating flange at either end. The second type, known as the 'single piece,' was used with the original four-speed (F4W71A) and automatic (3N71B) transmissions. The sliding portion on this shaft was built in

There are different designs of propshaft; this is a later one.

to the rear extension of the gearbox itself, and was lubricated with gear oil. As such, it featured only the rear four-bolt locating flange. Both types of propshaft were altered in mid-1971 as Nissan introduced a modification to reduce wear and vibration in the rear drivetrain. This was achieved by moving the differential gearbox rearwards to alter the operational angle of the two lateral driveshafts.

With the introduction of the new five-speed manual gearbox (FS5C71B) in January 1972, a feature of which moved the sliding portion into the transmission's rear casing, the need for a two-piece propshaft was negated and the type was withdrawn in mid-1972. If you experience some vibration and it is speed related, it might be due to a worn universal joint. They are straightforward to replace, although I don't recommend buying them from Nissan. Buy them straight from a supplier like GKN – they are much cheaper! Another popular conversion is to upgrade using UJs from Land Rover.

Rear axle
⁴ ³ ² ¹

The differential is held in place first by two vertical bolts, through a rubber insulated mounting bracket fitted to the rear suspension front crossmember, and via two

Nothing is covered (or protected).

horizontal studs on the crown wheel rear casing, to a moustache bar. This, in turn, is connected to the body via insulated Metalastic bushes, caps and two further vertical bolts on the rear chassis rails. An additional feature is the provision of a retaining strap, which fits over the pinion tunnel outer casing to arrest the torque reaction of the differential. The ratios are different depending on the gearbox configuration, and the ratios, unfortunately, cannot be identified from the outside. Many differentials have seen in excess of 250,000 miles, so they have demonstrated their strength, but they can be a little 'agricultural' by modern standards. Some models have had the later R200 (260Z) differential fitted with a 3.7:1 ratio, giving slightly more relaxed cruising. Rally cars can have up to a 5:1 ratio, which suits the shorter stages they run. Although Nismo manufactured limited slip diffs (LSDs), they are rare and valuable.

One modification that is becoming more popular is replacing the original 240Z differential with a Subaru R180 unit; it has the same 3.9 ratio, a limited slip diff (LSD) for improved handling, and is a good replacement. They will need face-plates for the half-shafts, but they do bolt direct onto the existing driveshafts. Other replacement options include units from the Nissan 200/240SX/Silvia, S13/14 and 15 models, and also upgrades from manufacturers like Quaife. The differential output shafts are connected, on four-bolt flanges, to the rear stub axles via a pair of driveshafts. Each shaft contains two universal joints and a sliding extension portion to compensate for the rear suspension movement. The stub axles are supported on two single-row ball bearings, spaced with a distance piece, at the bottom of each suspension strut.

Four-speed manual	3.364	Known as R180
Five-speed manual	3.900	–
Automatic	3.545	–

Front suspension

The front suspension on the 240Z utilises a modified version of the MacPherson strut design that was used on the Bluebird 510. The modification was a tension control rod that connected the track control arm to the chassis leg. Cars built up to June 1970 had a smaller lower ball joint that joined the steering arm to the strut/

Simple, independent layout.

track control arm. The original shock absorbers were of an integral design, but most have been replaced with a sealed cartridge type shock absorber, which Nissan introduced. The left and right suspension is connected by an anti-roll bar, which is a smaller diameter on the standard US domestic cars. The hard-type front suspension, fitted as standard to European models, was also available as an option in the US. So note that a standard US spec model will be sat higher and ride softer than a European specification car.

Rear suspension

The 240Z boasts an independent rear suspension (IRS) arrangement similar to the Chapman style from Lotus, that is unique to the S30s. In terms of handling it works very well by locating the rear wheels perpendicular to road at all times, irrespective of load. The downside is the noise generated in the cabin.

The front crossmember, which locates the differential, also locates the front mounting of the transverse link (A-frame) for either side of the suspension. The transverse link, or A-frame (because it looks like a capital A), connects to the base of the suspension leg via a long attachment spindle secured with a cotter pin. To save costs, Nissan only built one type – there are no 'left-hand' or 'right-hand' versions. From an engineering, production and cost viewpoint, this is a great idea, because the left-hand side A-frame is merely

The differential is secured at the front with a small crossmember, and at the back with the moustache bar.

Note that the left 'A frame' is upside-down and collects dirt.

mounted upside down. The problem is, because it is a pressed steel design, it collects dirt in the upturned part, meaning that the left-hand side A-frame has a tendency to rust much more quickly than the right-hand side. Make sure you check this.

The upper part of the suspension is the familiar MacPherson (Chapman) strut and any 'rebuildable' shocks have normally been replaced by cartridge type units (see front suspension). Although standard on RHD European models, 240Zs destined for other markets were not all fitted with an anti-roll bar, so don't panic if it's missing on the one you're looking at.

The A frames connect
to the independent
MacPherson struts.

Steering

[4] [3] [2] [1]

The 240Z was one of the first Japanese cars to feature rack-and-pinion steering, but there wasn't time to develop power steering, so all S30s were built unassisted; as such, steering effort is high, even on standard tyres. The rack-and-pinion system is simple and reliable, though most exhibit a little play in the straight ahead position.

The steering wheel can make a difference, both in terms of diameter and depth of the dish. Nissan didn't develop telescopically adjustable steering in time for production, so to offset different owner size, in what was designed as a 'world sports car,' different markets had steering wheels with varying depths of dish. European and US markets had a deep dished steering wheel; JDM (Japanese domestic market) models had a shallow dish. One interesting side note is that a shallow dish steering wheel brings it much closer to the indicator and lights/wiper stalks, which makes it possible to foul these when turning, and also inadvertently signal left or right.

One of the first
Japanese cars to
have rack-and-pinion
steering.

Brakes

[4] [3] [2] [1]

The servo-assisted braking setup for a 240Z consists of discs up front and drums at the rear, with the ⅞in tandem master cylinder/servo assembly mounted on the bulkhead. The dual braking system provides a separate circuit for both front and rear brakes. The twin reservoirs for this system are configured rear/front on master cylinders up to August 1971, and front/rear after that date. Pipes from the master cylinder connect to a shuttle valve, which, in the event of one circuit failing, will illuminate the brake warning lamp (the handbrake light).

Also incorporated is a proportioning valve that is designed to 'balance' braking, and prevent the rear brakes from locking up as the weight is transferred to the front of the car. This valve is located above the differential on models built up to June 1972; thereafter a redesigned unit was fitted to the bulkhead. This braking system revision also introduced the 7½in servo, which replaced the earlier 6in type.

The brake pipes were originally standard steel, held in metal clamps with rubber insulating blocks. These can suffer corrosion, and most have been replaced

Simple two-piston
caliper front brake.

Rear brakes use shoes,
not calipers, and have a
lightweight aluminium
drum with cooling fins.

with pipes of copper/kunifer. Beware, though – I've seen many with new pipes 'cable tied' to the old redundant pipes! The flexible pipes from the body to the brakes themselves were originally made of rubber, but have often been replaced by stainless steel. Squeaking brakes are normally caused by a dry backing plate (shim) on the front pads – an easy fix with copper-slip grease.

The front brakes, being discs, adjust automatically. The rear drums, however, have a form of automatic adjustability via the handbrake. When the handbrake is applied, it operates a lever which reacts on the slave cylinder. If the handbrake moves excessively, the lever rotates a screw that adjusts the shoes, which keeps the rear brakes set correctly. It does work, providing the handbrake cable is correctly adjusted.

Although the brakes are servo-assisted, it is often thought that the Z is a little under-braked, although a properly set up, standard system locks all four wheels!

The later 240Z (June 1972) has a bigger servo, but is not a direct replacement for the earlier example as some holes have to be realigned to fit. More popular is a caliper and disc upgrade, moving from a two-piston system to a four-piston system, either from Toyota or Range Rover. At the

The tandem brake master cylinder is on the left; the clutch master cylinder is on the right.

rear there are a number of conversions available, either using the setup from a 280ZX or even a 200SX. This, no doubt, improves the braking performance of a 240Z. If you do find any of these modifications, make sure you know what type it is and the parts used, so that you can at least get the right consumables.

Wiring loom

Compared with other 1970s vintage cars, the electrical system on a 240Z is vastly superior. Most sub looms use multiplugs that clip and lock together. This doesn't prevent corrosion of contacts, but does slow it down, and it is difficult to reconnect wires incorrectly as all of the major plugs have different design features or are colour coded. The current-load running via the fuse box and switches means a number of Zs have experienced 'burn outs' of the fuse box, so check the box for any evidence of melted plastic/overheating, or heat damage.

Although original fuse boxes were modified from 1971, replacement upgrades are now available. These are designed to plug into the original harnesses and utilise a printed circuit board with blade-type fuses. It also screws onto the original factory mountings. The essential issue is the amperage of the electrical system is not 'stepped down.' For example, the ammeter gauge displays a charging range up to +45 amps, the problem being that it is actually sending 45 amps to the gauge, instead of stepping it down to 10% – registering 45 amps but only sending 4.5 amps.

You can modify the headlamp wiring by

Most of the loom is a collection of multi-plugs and singular connectors.

incorporating relays, which effectively bypass the fuse box and headlamp switch. When fitted, the amperage is reduced from 20 amps to 5 amps, resulting in a lower load and much brighter lamps. Another upgrade is LEDs, again, offering much brighter lamps and a lower current load. If there is evidence that work like this has been carried out, it can be seen as a positive modification, if only in the interests of vehicle safety. Check for the not-so positive modifications, such as spot-lamps and alarm systems where wiring looms can be damaged and/or original plugs removed.

Wiring harnesses differed considerably depending on the destination market and model specification. Numerous changes were embodied throughout the S30's production, and to give a flavour of how many variations there are, below is a table of upgrades for the (non AUS) RHD manual HS30 model only.

Engine harness	Dashboard harness	Body harness
>12/70 - 24012-E4300	>12/69 - 24013-E4300	>12/70 - 24014-E4300
>06/72 - 24012-E4301	>09/70 - 24013-E4301	>06/72 - 24014-E4301
>07/72 - 24012-N3305	>12/70 - 24013-E4302	>07/72 - 24014_N3005
–	>08/71 - 24013-E8202	–
–	>06/72 - 24013-E8805	–
–	>12/72 - 24013-N3305	–

Wheels

240Zs were initially delivered to dealerships with the standard 4½in J steel wheels, with metal wheel covers. Most were upgraded to lighter alloy wheels, the most popular being Wolfrace in the UK. Alloy wheels do improve the looks and the handling of a 240Z. Once the car is on its third or fourth owner the aftermarket wheels would normally have grown in diameter and the tyre profile reduced. If this has been done in conjunction with lowering the car, then there can be a tendency

Most Zs now have aftermarket wheels.

for the wheels to foul the arches. A cheap fix is to bend the 'lip' of the arch back on itself which, while it fixes the issue, also makes a perfect breeding ground for rust.

If the car you are looking at has aftermarket/oversized wheels, check that they don't foul, and if possible, add some weight into the luggage area and have a passenger present for your test drive. Also check carefully that the wheel nuts used for the alloy wheels are the correct ones – not many cars drive well with three wheels! Larger or wider wheels will add weight to a steering system that is already heavier than average. This is compounded when a smaller steering wheel has also been fitted.

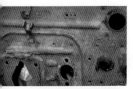 

The left bulkhead will rust wherever there is a weld ...

... and the same goes for the right-hand side.

Bulkhead

The bulkhead of the 240Z is a major area of rot and can be a difficult area to repair. Wherever the metal is welded to another panel there is a possible chance of rust. The battery tray is worth investigating, as batteries had a tendency to leak sulphuric acid. The chassis number is stamped on the upper driver's side of the bulkhead, so check that it matches with the number on the VIN plate located on the RHS inner wing.

There are two further plates on US market cars where the chassis number can be found: the first at the bottom of the windscreen on the driver's side and the second on the driver's door B-post, which also shows the production month and year.

Inner wings

The inner wings within the engine bay are a common area for rust, especially at the bottom where they meet the chassis rails. If repaired, try and make sure it's been done properly. Check the lower plating on the front suspension strut mount where it joins the inner wing. The upper part, where the suspension mount bolts through, is less likely to be affected. The reinforcing panel that sits underneath the outer wing is a target for road dirt, and the foam pad that is used between the top of this panel and the underside of the wing is perfect for cultivating damp and corrosion. Extensive use of your magnet will tell you a story.

Chassis and sills

A 240Z can, and will, if allowed, rot anywhere. A favourite area is the chassis legs. The combination of being directly in line of any dirt and grime coming up from the road, and a box section design that allows dirt to collect inside, causes the leg to rot from the inside out. Check every inch of the chassis leg, from the radiator crossmember to behind the front seats – particularly the front anti-roll bar mountings. The chassis leg is 'stepped' at the bulkhead as it goes underneath the floor. This is a strengthening area, and if it's rotten, it's bad news.

Once you've examined the legs, check the floorpans. They were initially built with rubber bungs which, if damaged or degraded, will harbour dirt and corrosion, or, if the bungs are missing, allow water into the floorpans and sound deadening material under the carpet. Lifting, looking and feeling the carpets will tell you what you need to know.

Inner and outer sills need to be carefully investigated, with many having had bodged repairs covered by underseal. Try and find out whether the treatment is there to protect, or to

The chassis leg is the main strength of the car, so check it thoroughly.

deceive. Check every welded joint and seam. The 240Z is mostly spot-welded, and was not seam-sealed, which means an unprotected weld is often the starting point for corrosion. Areas affected by this expand and distort as the corrosion bubbles through.

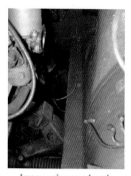

... and the underside of the car, too, if you can.

Inner wings: check both sides – from the top ...

The centre of the gearbox has a short crossmember, (rear engine mounting) fixed with three bolts, one centrally for the gearbox insulated mount, and two on either side of the transmission tunnel. The latter bolts were configured vertically up to July 1972, and horizontally thereafter. Cars after chassis number HS30-07501 featured a new mounting with two additional metalastic bushes. Ensure that this crossmember is solid, and that the bushes are in good condition.

Doors

Anywhere that dirt can collect and sit is ripe for corrosion, and the bottoms of doors are a favourite. Check along the bottom of the door skin and the bottom of the door for signs of damage. The door skin used to be a favourite for filler repairs, so use your magnet. Check that the window operates as it should, locates correctly in the frame when up, and does not rattle excessively when lowered into the door.

Check each door doesn't drop. If it does, the hinge pins and bushes will be worn, especially those in the upper hinges. Each door can have shims on each side of the hinges, although it is difficult to see if they are fitted. If the door is out of alignment missing shims may be the reason. However, if the door doesn't shut properly check, for badly adjusted latches. In extreme cases, the rear three-quarter panel may have been damaged and/or aligned badly during a repair.

The doors may let you out, but keep dirt and rust in!

A-pillars and rear arches

The windscreen of the 240Z is fitted with a rubber seal, that, if badly fitted, allows damp to sit between the rubber and the frame. This can lead to rotting of the A-pillar. This, together with blocked drainage from underneath the scuttle panel, produces the worst type of rot, from the inside, so check for leaks. The upper part of the inner rear arch is spot welded to the body; on some it reveals an almost perfect arc of rust bubbles. Repairs will have to be fixed from the inside out. Also check the sills as this is a common area for corrosion. Repair panels are available.

Headlamp surround – the early ones are made of GRP.

Headlamp surrounds

This is a potentially awkward area. Up to June '72 the headlamp cowls were made of GRP, the same material as the seats of swings. In fact, that's where the idea came from! So the cowl itself doesn't rot, but the connecting studs do! This means where the wing connects to the headlamp cowl they can, and will, snap or strip out if they are excessively rusted when you try to remove them. This is difficult to investigate, and will require getting your head under the front wheelarch.

Wings and valance

The good news is the wings of a 240Z are bolted, not welded. It has a series of bolts that run along the inside of the engine bay, under the scuttle and upper A-post.

At the front there is a bolt and captive nut that connects the wing to the front

The front valance bolts together like Meccano.

lower quarter valance, and three small nuts that connect the wing to the headlamp cowl. Then there are two bolts that locate the underside of the wing at the bottom behind the arch. Invariably, these bolts get everything the front tyre can throw at it. They are likely to be rusted and/or the area it bolts to may be missing, and the wing attached to the sill underneath by welding. As rust is systemic, the bottom of the wing in this area can also be poor, but at least you don't have to drill through any spot

welds to take it off (if as originally designed). As originally fitted, the front of the 240Z will have one of three variations of front valance:

● Up to June 1970, the car had a three-piece valance, a centre piece, bolted to the two front quarter valances with side-marker lights/indicators, fitted with either clear or amber lenses as markets dictated.

● From July 1970, a small rubber spoiler became available as an option. It was bolted to the three valance panels which were modified by adding captive nuts.

● The third type was a variation for the European market, where the optional spoiler was standard fitment, but due to height regulation restrictions, the indicators had to be moved from the front quarter valances; these new bespoke indicator units were mounted onto the front bumper, replacing the overriders.

B-pillar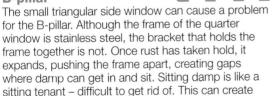

The small triangular side window can cause a problem for the B-pillar. Although the frame of the quarter window is stainless steel, the bracket that holds the frame together is not. Once rust has taken hold, it expands, pushing the frame apart, creating gaps where damp can get in and sit. Sitting damp is like a sitting tenant – difficult to get rid of. This can create corrosion around the frame and on the B-pillar.

The rear quarter window can hide rust in the B-pillar.

Bonnet 4 3 2 1

The bonnet hinges are at the front and use quite a substantial bracket attached to the inner wings located in front of the radiator support panel. The bonnet is a double-skinned unit, and a number of cars suffered a small dent right on the nose as it appears to be out of sight from the driver and is a victim of small parking mishaps. If it isn't addressed immediately and rot sets in, it can be difficult to fix because of the second skin.

Bonnet and hinges are substantial.

Hatchback 4 3 2 1

The hatchback provides a collection area at the bottom for dirt and moisture, and is an area to check for rot. The slam panel can also suffer as water draining down the side of the hatch aperture has nowhere else to go; water tends to pool in either corner by the rear quarters. There are two types of hatch. Models built up to December '70 do not have a rear spoiler, and the cabin air extraction is via a pair of vents mounted in the hatch and exiting just below the rear window. This was a design fault (allowing exhaust fumes to enter the car when decelerating) so many are now blocked off.

The slam panel, being flat, holds water until it rusts through.

From January 1971, the cabin ventilation system was modified with the ducting in the tailgate being deleted and re-routed to exit behind the redesigned Z emblem on the rear three-quarter panels. The rear spoiler, available from the same time, was optional in all markets except Europe, where it was standard fitment. Emblems previously on the tailgate were relocated to the new spoiler. There is only one strut, on the left-hand side, to hold up the hatch. If a pair are fitted, the tailgate is from a later model 260Z.

Rear panel 4 3 2 1

The further rearward you go on a 240Z, so the rust issues lessen, slightly. The rear panel constitutes the area between the rear light apertures, and includes the rear valence with integral central bumper section mounting points. This panel is protected from the elements to a certain extent by the fuel tank, therefore the panel behind the lights rarely suffers from corrosion, which is just as well, as replacements are no longer available. The biggest danger here is a rear end shunt, so it's worth keeping an eye on what's behind you as well as what's in front.

Roof 4 3 2 1

With the exception of the drain gulleys and corners, the roof of a 240Z shouldn't suffer too badly from corrosion. Weather damage, from hail for example, can affect some cars, but the main issue is when an aftermarket sunroof has been fitted. There are two types: the glass pop-up type popular in the 1980s, and the

Check the gutters.

older, more-in-keeping Webasto type. Both have stories of leaks, and in most cases there is a desire to return the Z to standard. If a sunroof exists (and the current owner allows) throw a bucket of water on top to check for leaks. It sounds extreme, but stopping leaks is a notoriously difficult thing to do. To check whether a sunroof has

Check the profile of the roof.

been removed, examine the roof panel's contours on both sides, and check the roof lining – it should be a simple, one-piece PVC lining with a small amount of padding, not an aftermarket design, such as velour or fur.

Not much brightwork, but what there is, suits the 240Z well.

Brightwork ④ ③ ② ①

Some of the brightwork on the 240Z is very long lasting. The gutter trim, rear quarter window and upper door frames boast stainless steel construction, and as such, they'll just need cleaning. It's the same for the trim around the front and rear screens. However, these are easily damaged if not removed and fitted correctly.

Although the bumpers are made of quite thick gauge steel, the application of the chrome was very poor, particularly on later replacement parts, and if it hasn't been reapplied it will look very tired by now. European legislation dictated that the number plate lamps be mounted on the bumper below the registration plate. The application of chrome on the unit that housed the repositioned lamps was extremely poor and on quite thin metal, and consequently didn't last long. For other markets, the rear number plate light sits above the number plate in a plastic housing. As a side note, although inoperative, the light mounting above the number plate was not deleted on the European model.

Badges and decals ④ ③ ② ①

On all but the earliest models the badges are chrome over plastic – the very early badges were a zinc-alloy metal, and, although they didn't rust, the chrome and paint would flake. Emblems did vary on the S30 series representing differing models and markets, but on the 240Z remained relatively constant. However, in January '71 the rear three-quarter emblem changed from '240Z' to a round badge with a 'Z' in the centre. Badges tend to be available online, and most have two or three pins that are supposed to clip into the bodywork. For the sake of a lost badge, I would advise to use double-sided tape as well.

Spoilers ④ ③ ② ①

From July 1970, a small rubber-like front spoiler became available as an option. Made of a flexible material, it was bolted to the three lower valance panels which were modified by adding captive nuts. The spoiler was added to stop the 240Z getting a floaty front end at higher speeds.

Most badges are chrome over plastic.

The rear spoiler applied to the tailgate was introduced in 1971 for the European specification model, and was an optional extra in other markets. Manufactured in cast polyurethane with a recess to access the tailgate lock assembly, it is fixed via six studs to the lower tailgate. Although reproductions exist, the originals are no longer available from Nissan; if they are available secondhand they may well be quite expensive.

A variety of aftermarket front spoilers are also available, of varying depths and widths, but this means one of two things: it's either part of a considered modification that is in keeping with other mods on the car, or it's a lash up, fitted to hide all manner of nasty surprises. Time to get on your back and check.

Some early and US models didn't have a rear spoiler.

Later UK models had a rear spoiler as standard.

Windows 4 3 2 1

The windscreen is of laminated construction, and was available in either clear or tinted form. The rear screen is made of toughened glass, as are the side windows.

Rear glass. Note the direction of the heating element.

There were two primary types of screen fitted during production. Until December 1971, the screen heating elements were, unusually, aligned vertically. From January 1972, the screen was modified to include the more traditional horizontally aligned elements. The rear glass was also available without heating elements, and came with options including clear, tinted, tempered and anti-sun variations. Most glass other than aftermarket windscreens is now only available secondhand, and prices are escalating.

Window rubbers 4 3 2 1

Even though original rubbers for the front and rear screen do appear to be available from Nissan, complete aftermarket rubber kits are available, and considerably cheaper. If you need to remove the glass and retain the screen intact, bear in mind that the best way to do it is to sacrifice the existing rubber. Using a sharp blade, cut from the inside and remove the screen first with the stainless steel trim still installed. Once out, remove the trim pieces gently – once the trim is damaged, it

Windscreen rubbers can harbour water – with horrible results.

will usually be irredeemable (the same applies to the tailgate). When refitting, after the new rubber is attached to the screen, it's best to fit the stainless steel brightwork to the rubber prior to installing the whole assembly in the car. Be aware that if the original was leaking you may have damage to repair before you can refit the screen.

Aftermarket window rubbers are available.

Headlamps [4] [3] [2] [1]

The 240Z originally used a standard sealed beam 7in lens with a paltry output of 45/55W. Many have been replaced with halogen bulbs as conversion kits were readily available some years ago. Although brighter, these bulbs increase the load on the fuse box and switch. A solution to this problem is to use relays or LEDs, which are reported to be 200% brighter but only require 25W.

Lighting was poor by today's standards. Upgrades are available.

On European models, the indicators sit atop the bumpers and replace the overriders, with the sidelights being part of the headlights. The indicators and side/marker lights on non-European models sit below the bumper, and are set in the front quarter valances. Dependent on market destination/regulation they can be: clear (using a twin filament 380 bulb), amber (using a 382-type bulb) or a twin-bulb configuration. Many owners of European-spec cars revert theirs to having the indicators below the bumpers, believing it looks much better.

Light clusters [4] [3] [2] [1]

The rear light clusters discolour over time, and US-sourced models have red/white against the RoW models, which are red/amber/white.
• Reversing lights and indicators use a 382-type single filament 21W bulb on each side.
• Rear lights use two 380-type, twin filament 5/21W bulbs on each side. Although aftermarket light clusters are available, the original items tend to be expensive.

Neat and tidy rear cluster houses five bulbs.

Dashboard [4] [3] [2] [1]

The 240Z dashboard is a single moulded piece, manufactured using a thermo-vacuum forming process, attached to a sheet metal frame. All are black, comprising two cowls in front of the driver, housing the speedo and rev counter. The top of the centre console houses three further gauges, and the glove box is lockable. The resin used in the dashboard is affected by consistent exposure to the sun – not a problem in the UK, but a lot of US/AUS sourced cars will have cracked dashboards where the resin has dried out. These can be repaired, and there are a number of YouTube videos that show how, but the dashboard would still need to be removed from the car.

Centre console [4] [3] [2] [1]

There are two types of centre console. Earlier models manufactured up to July 1971 have the ashtray set ahead of the gearlever, later cars have the ashtray behind the

gearlever, as it was deemed easier to access. Models built up to August 1971 have the choke lever set centrally behind the gearlever, and models built prior to February 1970 also had a hand throttle. Safety concerns in the US led Nissan to advise dealers to retrospectively remove this feature, as it was reported that the hand throttle was being used as a form of cruise control! Post-August 1971 models have the ashtray set behind the gearbox, and the choke lever is set on the left edge of the centre console. From April 1972, an optional lid was made available for the rear storage areas of the centre console.

The handbrake, with warning light switch, is set on the right-hand side of the tunnel, whether it is RHD or LHD.

Early design has the ashtray ahead of the gearlever. Later models have it behind.

Instruments

Atop the central dashboard area are the iconic three recessed cowls. The one furthest from the driver is the clock, which rarely works accurately! In the middle is

Simple, driver-focused instruments.

a split gauge, with the ammeter above and the fuel gauge below, and the nearest one to the driver is also a split gauge with the engine temperature gauge above and the oil pressure gauge below.

Most of the instruments are quite reliable. The speedo is cable operated, connecting directly to the gearbox. The rev counter is electronically driven.

Sometimes the fuel gauge can stop working – this is highly likely due to the connections on the back of the fuel tank or the variable resistor inside the tank. The most unreliable instrument is the clock, and you'll be lucky to find one that works accurately. The electro-mechanism often fails, normally due to the little electric motor that winds it.

Early model speedometers begin at 20mph, but complaints from US drivers meant this was changed to 10mph for later models.

The three – now iconic – central gauges.

Aftermarket quartz upgrades are available. The instrument lighting can be somewhat haphazard, as the clips that hold the bulbs in place on the back of the dials also act as the earth, and sometimes it's not a great connection. On cars with a 120psi gauge, it is not unusual for the oil pressure to almost read 0psi at idle when warm, but it should immediately move when the car is revved. Later cars were fitted with a 90psi gauge to rectify this problem. Oil pressure indication problems could also be due to the sender, as it sits below the oil filter and can get coated during servicing. Models built up to December 1970 had speedometers that start at 20mph!

Heater ▣ ▣ ▣ ▣

The heater control comprises a three-lever system with a three-speed fan. The top lever controls the option for fresh air ventilation, or air via the heater.

The middle lever is the temperature control, the bottom lever is for directional control – either ROOM or DEF – and the heater fan is situated under the dashboard on the passenger side, normally just about visible. Heater controls and installation are reversed on LH and RH drive cars.

Simple design heater controls – but difficult to understand!

Interior trim ▣ ▣ ▣ ▣

This is where it can get expensive. The trim on the door cards went through a stage of 'not being available' from Nissan, to 'being available,' and back to 'NBA.' The backing

The trim on the door cards can be tricky to find, and expensive.

is made of thick card with a PVC covering. The covers for the rear arches and side of the transmission tunnel are a plastic material with a moulded diamond shaped pattern. The roof lining is a smooth PVC with a thin foam backing, as are the A-pillars and roof support rails.

In the luggage compartment, there are two relatively complex moulded rear quarter panels, which are quite thin and fragile. Unfortunately, they were a favourite place to put additional speakers, so restoring a car to original condition might involve scouring

certain auction sites and being very lucky. I have seen them go for ●100s.

The rear quarter light and rear luggage bay panel are of a similar construction, and the latter has access panels to the rear light clusters. All these panels are fitted with colour coded plastic rivets. Replacement centre consoles are also becoming expensive, especially for what they are. Replacement carpets are available from a number of outlets for the 240Z. There were three primary interior colours, although the majority were black, but if you can find a car with either a tan or the very rare and sought-after peacock blue interior, I would consider it carefully.

Luggage compartment ▣ ▣ ▣ ▣

The luggage area is vast and makes the 240Z a very practical classic car. The hatch opens wide, on a single strut – check that it is strong enough to hold up the hatch.

There are two built-in longitudinal retaining straps, designed to hold luggage in place whilst driving. Underneath the carpet at the rear of the car is the spare wheel well.

If the car you are looking at has only four alloy wheels, make sure you have the correct nuts in case you need to use the spare, because they are unlikely to have the same type of seating. Check under the spare wheel for any signs of corrosion.

At the front of the luggage area on later models, the carpet should be 'cut' to provide access to two cubby holes situated behind each seat: each has a hinged metal cover, and can be closed (but not locked). The early models don't have these, but have two (fragile) plastic covers situated vertically behind each seat. These were designed to house the scissor jack and tool roll. At the very rear of the luggage area is a full width panel with two inspection covers, held in by four screws. These provide access to the rear light bulbs. Some owners fit a bracing strut between the suspension turrets. If the one you are looking at has one, this is definitely an aftermarket option.

A truly cavernous luggage space!

Evaluation procedure

Add up the total points
Score
• 172 = excellent (possibly concours)
• 129 = Good
• 86 = Average
• 43 = Poor

Cars scoring over 120 will be completely usable and will require only maintenance and care to preserve condition. Cars scoring between 43 and 88 will require some serious work or full restoration. Cars scoring between 89 and 119 will require very careful assessment of the necessary repair and restoration costs in order to arrive at a realistic value.

It is always worth bearing in mind what type of 240Z you want it to be at the end of this process, and it's recommended that you buy the very best you can afford, as it will be cheaper than the restoration costs involved in resurrecting a Z.

10 Auctions
– sold! Another way to buy your dream

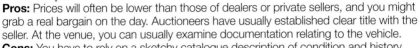

Auction pros & cons
Pros: Prices will often be lower than those of dealers or private sellers, and you might grab a real bargain on the day. Auctioneers have usually established clear title with the seller. At the venue, you can usually examine documentation relating to the vehicle.
Cons: You have to rely on a sketchy catalogue description of condition and history. The opportunity to inspect is limited, and you cannot drive the car. Auction cars are often a little below par and may require some work. It's easy to overbid. There will usually be a buyer's premium to pay in addition to the auction hammer price.

Which auction?
Auctions by established auctioneers are advertised in car magazines and on the auction houses' websites. A catalogue, or a simple printed list of the lots for auctions might only be available a day or two ahead, though often lots are listed and pictured on auctioneers' websites much earlier. Contact the auction company to ask if previous auction selling prices are available, as this is useful information (details of past sales are often available on websites).

Catalogue, entry fee and payment details
When you purchase the catalogue of the vehicles in the auction, it often acts as a ticket allowing two people to attend the viewing days and the auction. Catalogue details tend to be comparatively brief, but will include information such as 'one owner from new, low mileage, full service history,' etc. It will usually show a guide price to give you some idea of what to expect to pay, and will tell you what is charged as a 'Buyer's premium.' The catalogue will also contain details of acceptable forms of payment. At the fall of the hammer, an immediate deposit is usually required, the balance payable within 24 hours. If the plan is to pay by cash, there may be a cash limit. Some auctions will accept payment by debit card. Sometimes credit or charge cards are acceptable, but will often incur an extra charge. A bank draft or bank transfer will have to be arranged in advance with your own bank, as well as with the auction house. No car will be released before *all* payments are cleared. If delays occur in payment transfers, then storage costs can accrue.

Buyer's premium
A buyer's premium will be added to the hammer price: *don't* forget this in your calculations. It is not usual for there to be a further state tax or local tax on the purchase price and/or on the buyer's premium.

Viewing
In some instances it's possible to view on the day, or days before, as well as in the hours prior to, the auction. There are auction officials available who are willing to help out by opening engine and luggage compartments and to allow you to inspect the interior. While the officials may start the engine for you, a test drive is out of the question. Crawling under and around the car as much as you want is permitted, but you can't suggest that the car you are interested in be jacked up, or attempt to do the job yourself. You can also ask to see any documentation available.

11 Paperwork
– correct documentation is essential!

The paper trail
Classic, collector and prestige cars usually come with a large portfolio of paperwork, accumulated and passed on by a succession of proud owners. This documentation represents the real history of the car, and from it can be deduced the level of care the car has received, how much it's been used, which specialists have worked on it, and the dates of major repairs and restorations.

All of this information will be priceless to you as the new owner, so be very wary of cars with little paperwork to support their claimed history.

Registration documents
All countries/states have some form of registration for private vehicles, whether its like the American 'pink slip' system or the British 'log book' system.

It is essential to check that the registration document is genuine, that it relates to the car in question, and that all the vehicle's details are correctly recorded, including chassis/VIN and engine numbers (if these are shown).

If you are buying from the previous owner, his or her name and address will be recorded in the document: this will not be the case if you are buying from a dealer.

In the UK, the current (Euro-aligned) registration document is named 'V5C,' and is printed in coloured sections of blue, green and pink. The blue section relates to the car specification, the green section has details of the new owner, and the pink section is sent to the DVLA, in the UK, when the car is sold. A small section in yellow deals with selling the car within the motor trade.

In the UK, the DVLA will provide details of earlier keepers of the vehicle, upon payment of a small fee, and much can be learned in this way.

If the car has a foreign registration, there may be expensive and time-consuming formalities to complete. Do you really want the hassle?

Roadworthiness certificate
Most country/state administrations require that vehicles are regularly tested to prove that they are safe to use on the public highway and do not produce excessive emissions. In the UK, that test (the 'MoT') is carried out at approved testing stations, for a fee. In the USA, the requirement varies, but most states insist on an emissions test every two years as a minimum, while the police are charged with pulling over unsafe-looking vehicles.

In the UK, the test is required on an annual basis once a vehicle becomes three years old. Of particular relevance for older cars is that the certificate issued includes the mileage reading recorded at the test date and, therefore, becomes an independent record of that car's history. Ask the seller if previous certificates are available.

Without an MoT, the vehicle should be trailered to its new home, unless you insist that a valid MoT is part of the deal. (Not such a bad idea, this, as at least you will know the car was roadworthy on the day it was tested – and you don't need to wait for the old certificate to expire before having the test done.)

Road licence

The administration of every country/state charges some kind of tax for the use of its road system, the actual form of the 'road licence' and, how it is displayed, varying enormously country to country and state to state.

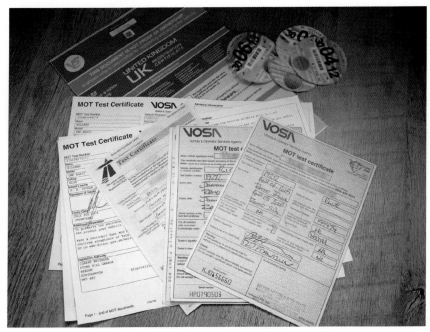

Take time to look through the car's paperwork.

Changed legislation in the UK means that the seller of a car must surrender any existing road fund licence, and it is the responsibility of the new owner to re-tax the vehicle at the time of purchase and before the car can be driven on the road. It's therefore vital to see the Vehicle Registration Certificate (V5C) at the time of purchase, and to have access to the New Keeper Supplement (V5C/2), allowing the buyer to obtain road tax immediately.

If the car is untaxed because it has not been used for a period of time, the owner must inform the licensing authorities, otherwise the vehicle's date-related registration number will be lost and there will be a painful amount of paperwork to get it re-registered.

Whatever the form of the 'road licence,' it must relate to the vehicle carrying it and must be present and valid if the car is to be driven on the public highway legally. The value of the license will depend on the length of time it will continue to be valid.

In the UK, if a car is untaxed because it has not been used for a period of time, the owner has to inform the licensing authorities, otherwise the vehicle's date-related registration number will be lost and there will be a painful amount of paperwork to get it re-registered. Also, in the UK, vehicles more than 40 years old qualify for free road fund licence – you must still apply in the normal way, but the cost is zero. Car clubs can often provide formal proof that a particular car qualifies for this valuable concession.

Certificates of authenticity

For many makes of collectible car, it is possible to get a certificate proving the age and authenticity (eg engine and chassis numbers, paint colour and trim) of a particular vehicle, these are sometimes called 'Heritage Certificates' and, if the car comes with one of these, it is a definite bonus. If you want to obtain one, the relevant owners' club is the best starting point.

If the car has been used in European classic car rallies, it may have a FIVA (Federation Internationale des Vehicules Anciens) certificate. The so-called 'FIVA Passport,' or 'FIVA Vehicle Identity Card,' enables organisers and participants to recognise whether or not a particular vehicle is suitable for individual events. If you want to obtain such a certificate go to www.fbhvc.co.uk or www.fiva.org; there will be similar organisations in other countries, too

Valuation certificate

Hopefully, the vendor will have a recent valuation certificate, or letter signed by a recognised expert stating how much he, or she, believes the particular car to be worth (such documents, together with photos, are usually needed to get 'agreed value' insurance). Generally such documents should act only as confirmation of your own assessment of the car, rather than a guarantee of value, as the expert has probably not seen the car in the flesh. The easiest way to find out how to obtain a formal valuation is to contact the owners' club.

Service history

Often these cars will have been serviced at home by enthusiastic (and hopefully capable) owners for a good number of years. Nevertheless, try to obtain as much service history and other paperwork pertaining to the car as you can.

Naturally, dealer stamps, or specialist garage receipts score most points in the value stakes. However, anything helps in the great authenticity game, items like the original bill of sale, handbook, parts invoices and repair bills, adding to the story and the character of the car. Even a brochure correct to the year of the car's manufacture is a useful document, and something that you could well have to search hard to locate in future years. If the seller claims that the car has been restored, then expect receipts and other evidence from a specialist restorer.

If the seller claims to have carried out regular servicing, ask what work was completed, when, and seek some evidence of it being carried out. Your assessment of the car's overall condition should tell you whether the seller's claims are genuine.

Restoration photographs

If the seller tells you that the car has been restored, then expect to be shown a series of photographs taken while the restoration was under way. Pictures taken at various stages, and from various angles, should help you gauge the thoroughness of the work. If you buy the car, ask if you can have all the photographs, as they form an important part of the vehicle's history. It's surprising how many sellers are happy to part with their car and accept your cash, but want to hang on to their photographs! In the latter event, you may be able to persuade the vendor to get a set of copies made.

12 What's it worth?
– let your head rule your heart

Values of 240Zs have consistently been on the rise but, like most classic cars, below the very best, very famous and very rare models there is a variation in the values – some very good cars have been sold in the teens, and whilst some Samuris have been sold at auction for more than ●50k, others have struggled to reach their reserve of ●30k.

Desirable options/extras

Apart from rare JDM models, on the surface, there wasn't too much in the way of model variation in the S30 range. There was no LX, GLX or GHIA to choose from. Basically, the 240Z was exported with two trim levels.

The US standard model, (HLS30 U and AU) supplied with a four-speed manual or three-speed automatic gearbox respectively, was considered the base HLS30 model. Options like air-conditioning were not fitted at the factory, but retrofitted by the dealerships.

The standard European model (HS30-UQ) supplied with the five-speed manual gearbox was considered the luxury or 'L' version. With features like uprated suspension and spoilers included, options were restricted to dealer add-ons like alloy wheels. The UK models also had dealer fitted seatbelts and door mirrors supplied by UK manufacturers for Datsun UK.

There is a lot of mythology given to the Samuri models. Each were specced and dependent on customer requirements at the time. Bear in mind that if the Samuri actually has a racing history you could be looking at Trigger's broom!* And this brings up the whole different issue of originality. Suffice to say, if a car has been reshelled then that fact shouldn't be hidden, otherwise it could be construed as fraudulent.

Depending on what you want your 240Z to be, originality and condition are the most important factors financially. If you are keen on modifying a car with things like an engine transplant, then it would make sense to try and find a 'shell' to build up from. Taking an original survivor, especially an early example with patina and modifying it with a V8 and big wheels, would do no good for your finances or popularity in Z circles.

The following will affect the value and desirability of a Datsun 240Z:
• Factory specification. Originality and correct parts for the year.
• Matching numbers. The numbers on the VIN (inner wing, windscreen, door slam panel) should all match, and match the engine number.
• Period modification. Many cannot afford the real thing, so a period mod is the next best option. Again, beauty is in the eye of beholder. Some cars may have what appears to be riveted-on arches – the 240ZG had these from the factory, and some owners fit these as a period modification.
• Road tax. All HS30s are exempt from road tax charge.
• MoT. All HS30s are now exempt from the Ministry of Transport road test. It is still recommended, and it might help the sale of a 240Z if it has a current one.
• Colour. The 240Z is one of the few cars that is colour agnostic. In other words, a 240Z looks good in any colour, but any original Datsun-numbered colour should attract a premium. However, the Samuri colours of orange and bronze are also recognised.

Undesirable features

Most Zs have been modified in various ways. Often this is how an owner puts their own 'signature' on a car, and of course all mods are a matter of taste, but some will detract from the car's appeal.

• Sunroof. Some UK market 240Zs were fitted at the dealer with a Webasto style sliding sunroof when new. The consensus is that these are more acceptable than the aftermarket glass fitments.

• Poorly executed mods. Engine/gearbox mods that are unfinished, interiors that have been cut about.

• Suspicious identity. As the value continues to ascend, more 'chancers' will try their luck passing off a Z as something it might not be. Do your homework and use the owner's clubs to help if required.

• Cosmetic mods. The rule of thumb is that US models didn't have spoilers, European models did, but neither had big aerodynamic wings!

• Paint schemes. Many European owners are restricted to modifying the body only. Wild colours and metalflake should be avoided, unless of course that is your 'thing'.

Striking a deal

As houses are all about location, location, location, Zs are all about condition, condition, condition. Be suspicious – buyers normally are – a private seller will only be selling their Z if there is a damn good reason. Most would sell their other half before selling the Z!

• Take someone who knows about the cars and is emotionally detached (preferably a club member) from the potential transaction. They can be your conscience.

• Value is always in the eye of the beholder, age and provenance is only valuable if it is valuable to you. Be prepared to walk away, even if you travelled a long distance, with a trailer, if the car is a lot worse than promised, it will save you money in the long term.

• Do not succumb to perceived authority, always get a second or third opinion. If you do decide to buy take whatever spares are on offer, you may not get another chance.

* 'Trigger' is character from the BBC comedy series *Only Fools and Horses*. In one scene, in a café, after having been presented with an award for saving the council money, Trigger claims that he's had his road sweeper's broom for 20 years – then adds that the broom has had "17 new heads and 14 new handles".
"How can it be the same bloody broom then?" asks Sid, the café owner. Trigger produces a picture of himself and his broom, and asks: "what more proof do you need?"

www.velocebooks.com / www.veloce.co.uk
Details of all current books • New book news • Special offers • Gift vouchers • Forum

52

13 Do you really want to restore?
– it'll take longer and cost more than you think

Nissan designed the 240Z to be a popular sports car from the outset, but even the company underestimated the success and popularity of the car, especially in the US. Six months after the model was released, Nissan had to build a new factory to keep up with demand. Cost management ensured the S30 was profitable for Nissan, but doing this placed reliance on dealers to complete the pre-delivery process. Sadly, this meant that many cars left the dealership lacking the necessary protection from the ravages of winter.

Despite the number produced, many rusted away within the first ten years; others were botched and then re-botched to keep them on the road. They rusted anywhere and everywhere. The 1980s were particularly hard on the 240Z and values dropped to a few hundred pounds (I bought a few!). Backstreet mods with wings, arches and whatever engine was available were the order of the day, as was blacked-out brightwork and XR3i bumpers and mirrors!

I always recommend that prospective owners buy the very best car they can afford, as the rust you can see from the outside will only be a proportion of the rust you will have to deal with. You always spend more on buying and restoring a cheaper car than buying the more expensive car that needs little or no work.

The front valance, headlamp pods, front wings, bonnet, scuttle panel, doors and rear hatch are all bolt-on items, which is the good news. The bad news is that a lot of the panels are now difficult to get hold of.

Interior trim is scarce, fragile and expensive. Even an imported RHD model from Australia that's relatively rust-free may have a poor interior and cracked dashboard. Replacement RHD dashboards are extremely rare, nowadays.

Your decision whether or not to take on a 'project' depends on the depth of your pockets and/or your welding skills. Bear in mind that the more you cut back a car to get to good metal, the more likely it is that the structure will collapse before you have a chance to rebuild it. Plan your work accordingly, avoiding working on multiple structural areas at the same time without supporting jigs/fixtures. It is also worth noting that the restoration costs of any similar specification 240Z will be the same as restoring one that is rare or has history. So, pick the right car.

The L-series engine was used in a number of models within Nissan as well as in a number of kit cars and replicas, so spares are available. Buying a solid 240Z with a poor engine is a much better bet than buying a rotting pig with a sweet-sounding motor. Triple carb setups are four figures, so budget accordingly.

Buying a partly-restored model can be tricky, especially if it looks like all the hard work has been done. After all, would you sell something when you are on the downhill part of the restoration? Investigate it thoroughly: because it is partly dismantled it might be easier to see what is still on the 'to do' list.

Whilst a classic car is 'never finished,' many owners do a rolling restoration, enjoying the car in the summer and working on it in the winter. This can be quite a successful way of avoiding problems and keeping a 240Z on the road, working on one specific area at a time in the winter. A well-documented restoration is worth considering, if you can afford the initial outlay, especially if it is an original model, and comes with good quality photographs.

14 Paint problems
– bad complexion, including dimples, pimples and bubbles

Paint faults generally occur due lack of protection/maintenance, or to poor preparation prior to a respray or touch-up. Some of the following conditions may be present in the car you're looking at:

Orange peel
This appears as an uneven paint surface, similar to the appearance of the skin of an orange. The fault is caused by the failure of atomized paint droplets to flow into each other when they hit the surface. It's sometimes possible to rub out the effect with proprietary paint cutting/rubbing compound, or very fine grades of abrasive paper. A respray may be necessary, in severe cases. Consult a bodywork repairer/paint shop for advice on the particular car.

Orange peel – can be rectified – with work.

Cracking
Severe cases are likely to have been caused by too heavy an application of paint (or filler beneath the paint). Also, insufficient stirring of the paint before application can lead to the components being improperly mixed, and cracking can result. Incompatibility with the paint already on the panel can have a similar effect. To rectify the problem, it is necessary to rub down to a smooth, sound finish, before respraying the problem area.

Cracking – be vigilant when inspecting plastic panels or bumpers.

Crazing
Sometimes the paint takes on a crazed, rather than a cracked, appearance when the problems mentioned under 'Cracking' are present. This problem can also be caused by a reaction between the underlying surface and the paint. Paint removal and respraying the problem area is usually the only solution.

Blistering
Almost always caused by corrosion of the metal beneath the paint. Usually perforation will be found in the metal, and the damage will usually be worse than that suggested by the area of blistering. The metal will have to be repaired before repainting.

Blistering – tends to be localised.

Micro blistering
Usually the result of an economy respray where inadequate heating has allowed moisture to settle on the car before spraying. Consult a paint specialist, but, in most

cases, damaged paint will have to be removed before partial or full respraying. Can also be caused by car covers that don't 'breathe.'

Fading
Some colours, especially reds, are prone to fading, if subjected to strong sunlight for long periods without the benefit of polish protection. Sometimes proprietary paint restorers and/or paint cutting/rubbing compounds will retrieve the situation. Often a respray is the only real solution.

Peeling
Often a problem with metallic paintwork when the sealing lacquer becomes damaged and begins to peel off. Poorly applied paint may also peel. The remedy is to strip and start again!

Dimples
Dimples in the paintwork are caused by the residue of polish (particularly silicone types) not being removed properly before respraying. Paint removal and repainting is the only solution.

Dents
Small dents are usually easily rectifed by the 'Dentmaster,' or equivalent process, that sucks or pushes out the dent (as long as the paint surface is still intact). Companies offering dent removal services usually come to your home: consult the web/your telephone directory.

It's shiny on the outside – but is it shiny underneath and inside?

15 Problems due to lack of use
– just like their owners, 240Zs need exercise!

There are few things that are as bad for a car as lack of use, as this usually means it has been stored in a damp garage and forgotten about. Think twice about any Z that the owner has frequently started up for short periods 'just to see,' as this will produce a lot of moisture inside the engine and exhaust system, which will combine with other combustion products to form acids. These attack the silencers, timing chains, cam lobes, and other parts.

Brakes seize if not used for a while.

Brakes The car should ideally have been stored in gear, with the handbrake off, as inaction, particularly in damp conditions, can cause the clutch plates, brake pads and discs or handbrake shoes and drums to rust together. This is not as serious as it sounds: to free the clutch, simply start the engine with the brakes fully on, in fifth gear with the clutch pedal pressed (clutch disengaged).

To free the brakes, engage first or reverse gear, rev the engine a little, and slowly engage the clutch. The brakes usually come free with a loud bang.

Don't worry about a coating of rust on the discs, as this rapidly wears away. Give them plenty of use, and, if in doubt, replace the pads. If the brakes bind, lever the pads outwards against the discs, looking for stiffness indicative of the pads having rusted to their carrier bracket. Removal requires some effort, after which a light coat of Copper Slip or similar on the sliding surfaces restores and maintains normal action.

Battery So many enthusiasts neglect their battery for months on end. The associated sulphation is responsible for killing more batteries than anything else. Even an overnight charge will not compensate for the reduced capacity caused by this.

Fluids Brake fluid absorbs moisture, usually through the rubber hoses. Expect to replace the brake and clutch fluid very soon, bleeding it through the nipples until all the old fluid is purged. The use of a coloured fluid such as the ATE Blue Racing–type provides a useful indicator.

Tyres If the car has been resting on its tyres, expect some temporary vibration due to the inevitable flat spots this produces. Check the pressures – higher pressures reduce this effect. Remember that any tyre over ten years old will have hardened and lost a lot of its grip, particularly in wet conditions.

Rubber and plastic items Due to the high quality of the rubber-like and plastic materials used by Datsun, it is unusual to find any problems with hoses or window seals etc, which usually last the life of the car. A periodic application of WD40 or similar is a good practice, and it does no harm to run your fingers over all the cooling system hoses, checking for bulges, leaks or oil contamination.

16 The Community
– key people, organisations and companies in the 240Z world

Having been involved with the 240Z since 1985, I have seen the public opinion change, from regarding a car as 'Jap Crap' because it rusted, to it being on the receiving end of ignorant comments about German designers, Japanese manufacturers and the war, to now, where they are universally admired.

There are many areas where 240Zs are still active: road, circuit and drag racing, rallying, car shows and driving tours ... because of the varied uses, all tastes are catered for. The Zs claim that it is the best selling sports coupé in the world is not solely because of the 240Z.

The lineage stretches from: • 260Z (RS30) • 260Z 2+2 (GRS30) • 280Z (S30) • 280ZX (S130) • 300ZX (Z30/31) • 300ZX TT (Z32) • 350Z (Z33) • 370Z (Z34).

Each model was different from the last, whether through cost-cutting, market positioning or reinvention, and, rightly so, it has its own group of dedicated followers. The owners of each model are fiercely protective of their cars, and are happy to debate the pros and cons of each model in the lineage.

There is plenty of support for each model, bearing in mind that the UK was never one of the major markets for the Z series. Because of the numbers sold in the US, there are a greater number of suppliers Stateside. While there are specialists in the UK who focus on the Datsun Z, the construction of the car is quite straightforward and basic, so any restorer worth their salt will be able to complete the work to a good standard.

Personal recommendation is always the best way, as any specialist is only as good as the last job they have completed. So join a club – some offer a 'pre-purchase service' where they go with the buyer to investigate and advise, many offer forums, and there are a large number of Facebook pages dedicated to the S30.

Clubs and forums
You'll find the owners and club members a friendly bunch, always willing to talk 'Z' until the cows come home.

Classic Z Car Club (S30 & S130) www.classiczcars.com .
Classic Z Register (S30 only) www.s30.org
Cleveland Z Car Club (All models) www.clevelandzclub.com
Connecticut Z Car Club (All models) www.ctzcc.com
Datsun Register WA (S30) www.wazregister.com
Datsun 240Z, 260Z, 280ZX Club of Australia www.viczcar.com
Datsun France www.datsun-france.com
Datsun Z Club France www.datsunzclubfrance.free.fr
Datsun Nissan Sports Cars of Finland (All models) www.dnsf.org
Datsun Z Club Switzerland www.datsun-z-club.ch

Desert Z Association - Arizona (All models) www.desertzassociation.com

Edmonton Z Car Club (All models) www.edmontonzcarclub.com

Emerald City Z Club (All models) www.emeraldcityzclub.com

Fairlady Z Club France (S30 & S130) www.fairladyzclubfrance.com

Group Z (All models) www.groupz.com

Heart of America Z Car Club (All models) www.hazcc.com

Inland Empire Z Car Club of Southern California (All models) www.empirez.com

Maryland Z Car Club (All models) www.mdzclub.org

Middle Tennessee Z Club (All models) www.middletennesseezclub.com

New Jersey Z Car Club (All models) www.njzclub.com

Nissan Datsun Sports Car Club Inc (All models) www.ndsoc.com.au

Northwest Z Club www.northwestz.org

Oklahoma Z Car Club www.okzcc.com

Ontario Z Car Owners (All models) www.ontariozcar.com

Thread Doctor Services www.threaddoctorservicesltd.co.uk

Triad Z Club www.triadzclub.com

Triangle Z Club (All models) www.trianglezclub.com

Upstate Z Club (All models) www.upstatezclub.com

Windy City Z Club (All models) www.windycityzclub.com

Z Association of New York (All models) www.zanyz.com

Z Car and Roadster Owners Club (All models) www.zroc.org

Z & ZX Club Deutschland (All models) www.z-zx-club.de

Z & ZX Club of Holland (All models) www.z-zxclub.nl

Z Car Club of Colorado (All models) www.zccc.org

Z-Car Club Of Inland Valley (All models) www.zcciv.co

Z Car Club of Queensland (All models) www.zcarclubq.org.au

Z Car Club of Rochester (All models) www.zccr.net

Z Car Club of Washington (All models) www.zccw.org

Z Car Club of Sydney www.zcarclub.com.au

Z Club of Great Britain (All models) www.zclub.net

Z Club of San Diego www.zcsd.org

Z Club of Texas www.zcluboftexas.org

Z Owners of Northern California www.zonc.org
Z Club NZ www.zclub.nz
ZZZing Network www.zzzing.net
Specialists, parts and modifications
Arizona Z Car www.arizonazcar.com
Car Parts Manual www.carpartsmanual.com
Fourways Engineering www.fourways-engineering.co.uk
Mike's Z Shop www.mikeszshop.com
MJP Eastern Auto www.mjpauto.com
The Z Store www.thezstore.com
Vintage Z Parts www.vintagezparts.com
Xenon Z Car www.xenonzcar.com
Z Car Parts www.zcarparts.com
Z Clocks www.zclocks.com
Z Farm www.thezfarm.co.uk
Zedd Findings www.datsunzparts.com
ZeddSaver www.zeddsaver.com
Z Specialties www.zspecialties.com

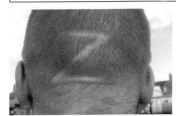

Enthusiasm knows no bounds!

One of the few cars that look good in any colour.

17 Vital statistics
– essential data at your fingertips

Engine
S30 – 2.0: 1952cc; six-cylinder; OHV; 12-valve; 115bhp; 112lb-ft
HS30 – 2.4: 2393cc; six-cylinder; OHV; 12-valve; 151bhp; 146lb-ft
PS30 – 2.0: 1989cc; six-cylinder; DOHC; 24-valve; 160bhp; 130lb-ft

Transmission
Four-speed manual; rear wheel drive; final drive 3.364:1
Five-speed manual; rear wheel drive; final drive 3.900:1
Three-speed automatic; rear wheel drive; fFinal drive 3.545:1

Suspension
Front: Independent with MacPherson struts, lower transverse link and tie rod, shock absorbers, coil springs and anti-roll bar.
Rear: Independent with Chapman struts, transverse link, shock absorbers, coil springs and optional anti-roll bar.

Brakes
Front: 10.7in (270mm) discs
Rear: 9.0in (230mm) x 1.6in (41mm) drums

Steering
Rack and pinion, 2.7 turns lock to lock

Wheels
4.5J-14 steel wheels with metal trims and 175SR14 tyres

Dimensions
Length: 4136mm (162.8in)
Width: 1630mm (64.1in)
Wheelbase: 2305mm (90.7in)
Height: 1283mm (50.5in)
Weight: 1044kg (2300lb)

Production figures

Year	USA	Canada	Australia	UK	Others
1970	16,215	1201	319	2	3
1971	33.684	3440	894	264	89
1972	52,628	4020	362	549	494
1973	45,588	2537	783	1114	430
Totals	**148,115**	**11,198**	**2358**	**1929**	**1016**

The "Others" column include 240Zs sold into Germany (112), Holland (232) and France (672). However, total production figures from Nissan for the 240Z were declared as 164,616 units. This contradicts the totals quoted in the table above when added together of 168,584. The discrepancy of 3968 units could be due to one or both of the following.

Discrepancy #1
One explanation is that some of the first 260Zs built in the last quarter of 1973 were included in the larger total amount of 168,584 units. But also see below.

Discrepancy #2
According to the final edition of the RHD Nissan S30 parts catalogue, dated December '79, the last chassis number is declared as HS30-101537. It is known for certain that several cars in the UK have chassis numbers quoting HS30-103xxx. This shows an error of at least 1500 unaccounted units that, according to the Nissan publication, were not built!

One of these is worth two or three times more than the other.

The holy grail – the Z432.

Index